FAT AND BLOOD

CLASSICS IN GENDER STUDIES

Series Editor Michael S. Kimmel
Dept. of Sociology, SUNY at Stony Brook

Each generation of scholars rediscovers the "classics" that it needs. These works ground our contemporary research and provide historical context. What makes them "classics" is not simply that they're old, but that they continue to speak to contemporary concerns. Sadly, many brilliant works by major scholars and thinkers that were so influential in their time have passed out of print. The books in this series will reintroduce these works both to established scholars and to a new generation of students and researchers as they examine the origins of our understanding of contemporary gender relations.

BOOKS IN THE SERIES

The Home: Its Work and Influence, Charlotte Perkins Gilman (2002)
Reprint of the 1903 edition with an introduction by Michael S. Kimmel

Concerning Children, Charlotte Perkins Gilman (2003)
Reprint of the 1900 edition with an introduction by Michael S. Kimmel

His Religion and Hers: A Study of the Faith of Our Fathers and the Work of Our Mothers, Charlotte Perkins Gilman (2003)
Reprint of the 1923 edition with an introduction by Michael S. Kimmel

Fat and Blood; And How to Make Them, S. Weir Mitchell (2004)
Reprint of the 1882 edition with an introduction by Michael S. Kimmel

Wear and Tear; Or, Hints for the Overworked, S. Weir Mitchell (2004)
Reprint of the 1973 Arno Press reprint edition with an introduction by Michael S. Kimmel

ABOUT THE SERIES EDITOR

Michael S. Kimmel is professor of sociology at the State University of New York, Stony Brook. His publications include *The Politics of Manhood* (1996), *Manhood in America: A Cultural History* (1996), and *The Gendered Society* (2000). He is the current editor of the international, interdisciplinary journal *Men and Masculinities*.

Classics in Gender Studies Series
AltaMira Press
1630 North Main Street #367
Walnut Creek, CA 94596
(925) 938-7243
www.altamirapress.com

FAT AND BLOOD
AND HOW TO MAKE THEM

S. WEIR MITCHELL

EDITED AND INTRODUCED BY
MICHAEL S. KIMMEL

A Division of
ROWMAN & LITTLEFIELD PUBLISHERS, INC.
Walnut Creek • Lanham • New York • Toronto • Oxford

ALTAMIRA PRESS
A division of Rowman & Littlefield Publishers, Inc.
1630 North Main Street, #367
Walnut Creek, CA 94596
www.altamirapress.com

Rowman & Littlefield Publishers, Inc.
A wholly owned subsidiary of The Rowman & Littlefield Publishing Group, Inc.
4501 Forbes Boulevard, Suite 200
Lanham, MD 20706

PO Box 317
Oxford
OX2 9RU, UK

Introduction Copyright © 2004 by AltaMira Press

British Library Cataloguing in Publication Information Available

Library of Congress Cataloging-in-Publication Data

Mitchell, Silas Weir, 1829–1914.
  Fat and blood: and how to make them.
  Philadelphia, J.B. Lippincott company, 1878.
  1. Neurasthenia. 2. Hysteria. 3. Rest.
RC343.M6 1905   05029850

ISBN   978-0-7591-0675-8

Printed in the United States of America

⊖™ The paper used in this publication meets the minimum requirements of American National Standard for Information Sciences—Permanence of Paper for Printed Library Materials, ANSI/NISO Z39.48–1992.

INTRODUCTION.

MICHAEL S. KIMMEL

"THE real purpose of the story was to reach Dr. S. Weir Mitchell, and convince him of the error of his ways. I sent him a copy as soon as it came out, but got no response. However many years later, I met someone who knew close friends of Dr. Mitchell's who said he had told them that he had changed his treatment of nervous prostration since reading 'The Yellow Wallpaper.' If that is a fact, I have not lived in vain."[1]

So wrote Charlotte Perkins Gilman, perhaps the most influential feminist sociologist at the turn of the last century, and the author of the memorable short story, "The Yellow Wallpaper." In that story, Gilman describes how the "rest cure" prescribed by a

---

[1] Charlotte Perkins Gilman, *The Living of Charlotte Perkins Gilman, An Autobiography* [1935] New York: Harper and Row, 1975, p. 121.

well-known physician gradually drove a young woman into an unrecoverable madness, so that, by the end of the story, she only could see the terrifying floral patterns of the yellow wallpaper in the room that had become her prison.

It's well known that the story was based on Gilman's own experience of the "cure" prescribed to her for a mental breakdown following the birth of her daughter. Gilman, herself, described her first encounter with the great doctor in her *Autobiography*:

I was put to bed and kept there. I was fed, bathed, rubbed, and responded with the vigorous body of twenty-six. As far as he could see there was nothing the matter with me, so after a month of this agreeable treatment he sent me home, with this prescription:

'Live as domestic a life as possible. Have your child with you all the time. . . . Lie down an hour after each meal. Have but two hours' intellectual life a day. And never touch pen, brush, or pencil as long as you live.'

Gilman recounts that she "went home, followed those directions rigidly for months, and came perilously close to losing my mind."[2]

But who was this physician who prescribed a regi-

---

[2] Gilman, *The Living*, p. 96.

men so monstrous that its most famous patient recalled it as resulting, inevitably in "progressive insanity"?[3] How could his diagnosis have been so disastrously wrong?

In fact, S. Weir Mitchell was among the nineteenth century's most eminent physicians, a man of enormous literary and medical talents, whose influence was profound in many quarters, and who, at the turn of the century, jumped on a bandwagon of gender-hysteria that swept across American society.

His work on the etiology and treatment of neurasthenia, commonly called "brain drain," provided the intersection of medical diagnoses of a serious ailment with cultural critiques of modernity and the vigorous reassertion of traditional gender ideologies. It was for neurasthenia that Mitchell treated Gilman, and countless others, for whom the pace and pressures of modern society had proved too difficult to bear, and who were exhibiting symptoms ranging from severe depression and unbearable lassitude, to anxiety and panic disorders.

Neurasthenia was among the most gendered illnesses of the turn of the century. For both women and men, the cause was gender non-conformity, and

---

[3] Gilman, *The Living*, p. 119.

the cure was a rigorously enforced conformity to the "natural" activities appropriate for men or women. Men were afflicted because of too much work—desk work, brain work, the sedentary work of the middle-class white-collar office—that took men away from their hardy, outdoor-oriented pioneering spirit. And so, Mitchell and others prescribed the tonic freshness of the outdoors, the robust vigor of newly created "dude ranches"—masculine theme parks to enable men to retrieve their natural virility that had been sapped by the dreary tedium of the daily grind.

By contrast, society women suffering from neurasthenia were suffering from *too much* exertion, not too little. Again, a case of gender non-conformity as these women were doing too much, beyond what their bodies would naturally allow. So women were counseled to take to their beds, with nary a bodily movement and certainly no physical activity, for months on end.

This volume presents one of Mitchell's touchstone texts of this cultural critique as medical diagnosis. *Fat and Blood* was a best-seller in its time and went through multiple printings and numerous editions. It fused the cultural critique of modern society and the inversion of gender roles with the medical analysis of this strange new ailment.

INTRODUCTION.

Today we are likely to read it angrily, as it serves to enforce the most pernicious stereotypes about women (and not so incidentally, about men)— stereotypes that have proved resilient obstacles to women's advancement. Or we might read it ironically, as almost comic recitations of a cultural critique of modernity that has been all but superceded in the contemporary era. Some will be tempted to read it with the jaundiced eye of historical distance, as quaint anachronisms of a bygone era.

I think, however, that it supports another reading, a bit more contemporary and certainly more engaged. There are constant arguments that resound across more than the century since they were written. Fans, for example, of Robert Bly, *Fight Club*, "The Man Show," or *Stiffed* might recognize some of Mitchell's critiques of the masculine malaise, even if we don't especially share Mitchell's therapeutic interventions (just as, I imagine, most of us don't think that imaginary bare-knuckle fighting or watching big-breasted bikini-clad women bounce on trampolines is going to cure what ails us). And surely anti-feminists on the right will find contemporary support for curtailing women's employment or education as upsetting the naturally ordained order of things. And, of course, sufferers of chronic fatigue syndrome, that contemporary version of neurasthenia, will find both diagnosis and treatment options to sound painfully familiar.

More than that, though, are the small, quotidian ways in which we each partake in some morsel of the critique that Mitchell offers—from vitamin regimens and diligent calculation of food intake, to various therapies to add or subtract weight, bulk, or muscle. These ideas are hardly quaint and curious footnotes in medical and cultural history; rather they recycle themselves, and are deliberately recycled, in every generation, as each generation tries to understand how best to live in a world that, as Bruce Springsteen sang, "rips the bones from your back."

II.

Silas Weir Mitchell was born on February 15, 1829, the son of a physician who was a prominent member of the faculty at the Jefferson Medical College in Philadelphia.[4] Mitchell entered the college

---

[4] This brief biography is based on Ira Rutkow's introduction to *Gunshot Wounds and Other Injuries of Nerves* (San Francisco: Norman Publishing, 1989), Richard Walter, *S. Weir Mitchell, M.D. Neurologist: A Medical Biography* (Springfield, Ill.: Charles C. Thomas, 1970), and Joseph Lovering, *S. Weir Mitchell* (New York: Twayne, 1971).

department of the University of Pennsylvania in 1844 at age 15, but had to leave four years later when his father became ill, and, as the eldest son, young Silas had to help support the family. When his father recovered, Mitchell resumed his studies at Jefferson, from which he graduated in 1850.

In 1851, Mitchell joined his father's medical practice. In the years leading up to the Civil War, he undertook several research projects, especially on blood composition. The Civil War provided him with significant opportunities to develop his interest in neurology. Originally appointed acting assistant surgeon in the Union Army, he was eventually placed in charge of the Turner's Lane Hospital in Philadelphia. There, treating hundreds of battle-scarred and wounded veterans of the war, Mitchell undertook research on traumatic nervous injuries, especially on casualties from the Battle of Gettysburg. Based on this research, he wrote *Gunshot Wounds and Other Injuries of Nerves* (1864), one of the path-breaking medical texts of the century.

This was followed in 1872 with *Injuries to Nerves and Their Consequences*. Here he made an eloquent case for the lingering psychological and physical effects of nerve injury. "Under such torments the temper changes, the most amiable grow irritable, the soldier becomes a coward, and the strongest man is scarcely less nervous than the most hysterical girl," he wrote. [5]

These early books and scientific articles were decidedly medical in nature, and attended to the physiology of nerves. By the mid-1870s, though, he began to turn his attention to cultural criticism in the guise of medical treatise. *Wear and Tear* appeared in 1871; here he argued that Americans are incapable of play, and predicted an increase in nervous disorders. *Wear and Tear* became a best-seller, a popular general treatise on culture and mental and physical health, and brought Mitchell significant public attention. *Fat and Blood; and How to Make Them* followed soon after (1877).

Mitchell built on his newfound fame to write two major general neurology textbooks, *Lectures on the Diseases of the Nervous System, Especially in Women* (1881) and *Clinical Lessons on Nervous Diseases* (1897). These works made him, perhaps, the most famous neurologist of the nineteenth century, and certainly one of the most eminent physicians of the time.

---

[5] S. Weir Mitchell, *Injuries of Nerves and their Consequences* (Philadelphia: J. B. Lippincott, 1872), p. 196.

INTRODUCTION.   xiii

In these and other works, Mitchell revealed an abiding interest in hysteria and much of these treatises were devoted to its description and treatment. Having helped to establish neurology as a medical specialty, he was also critical of contemporary asylums and institutional psychiatry at the turn of the century. He condemned the treatment of the insane as barbaric.

In all, Mitchell wrote more than 170 medical and scientific papers. He was the first president of the Congress of American Physicians and Surgeons and was elected a trustee at the University of Pennsylvania, where he had been earlier rejected as a professor.

Interestingly, Mitchell is perhaps as well known today as a second-tier novelist and poet, as he is as a physician. At age 20, he recounted that he sent a volume of poetry to a Boston publisher, who rejected the submission on the advice of Oliver Wendell Holmes. Holmes advised Mitchell to continue his medical career before turning to literature. Mitchell followed this advice, and only began publishing poetry in the 1880s. Several volumes of poetry followed quickly.

He also published fourteen novels. Best known among these were the five novels which took the

Civil War as their backdrop, including *In War Time*, first published as a serial in twelve installments in *The Atlantic* in 1884; *Hugh Wynne* (1896), his most popular book; and *Westways* (1913), his last novel. A short story "The Case of George Dedlow," published in *The Atlantic* in 1866, fused his medical knowledge with his desire to write fiction. Mitchell chronicles the saga of a young man, who, as a result of war injuries, had both his arms and legs amputated, leaving him with only a torso. In the first known written account of phantom limb pain, Mitchell wrote that he continued to "feel" his missing limbs.

In 1888, he received an honorary doctorate from Harvard at the 250th commencement. He counted William Dean Howells and James Russell Lowell as his friends. His ideas influenced Freud, who favorably reviewed his work and later adapted some measure of the rest cure in his own practice. One story that Mitchell was fond of telling indicates both his humor and vanity. In France, Mitchell visited the great physician Jean-Martin Charcot, who would later train Freud in medicine. When Mitchell arrived at Charcot's office, instead of being formally announced, he asked the secretary to present to Charcot a patient suffering from a host of imaginary ailments. She also informed Charcot that this patient was soon leaving for America. When she relayed this condition to Charcot, he recommended that the patient postpone treatment until he could be seen by Dr. S. Weir Mitchell in America!

Mitchell married Mary Cadwalader in 1875 and they had one daughter who died in early adolescence. S. Weir Mitchell died in 1914 and is buried in Philadelphia.

III.

Mitchell's own life provides a rough parallel for much of his work. Growing up in the shadow of a prominent physician father, he took to heart his father's admonition that his son had the talent to succeed, but lacked the persistence necessary to survive the rigors of a medical education. "My father's words greatly troubled me," he wrote later. "I had a conscience which did, and has had to do, much work. I was always failing from lack of energy and always penitent . . ."[6]

And like other self-made men of the era, most no-

---

[6] Anna Robeson Burr, *Weir Mitchell, His Life and Letters* (New York: Duffield, 1929), p. 44.

tably Theodore Roosevelt, Mitchell remade himself in the mold he had fashioned for himself, finding reserves of energy and perseverance that he had feared were lacking.

While it is tempting to see Mitchell's interest in the chronic fatigue syndrome of the turn of the last century as the direct consequence of his own persistent self-criticism of his lassitude and lack of energy, I think it is probably more accurate to see it as the progression of his work on the physiology of nerve injuries in the Civil War to those apparently nervous symptoms that had no immediately apparent etiology. In touch with the prevailing cultural currents of the era, Mitchell understood nervous debility to stem directly from modern life.

The fusion of cultural critique and medical diagnosis is evident in *Fat and Blood*. Mitchell adumbrates the essential physiological elements of treatment as much as medical diagnoses of the ailments. The subtitle *and How to Make Them* immediately announces a pragmatic treatise, although his discussion of the "rest cure" makes clear that it is as essential to change the "moral atmosphere" of the patient as it is the physical condition.

Politically, he begins by lamenting the "incessant feebleness" of the female sex and the myriad examples of hysteria he has witnessed and treated. To be sure, men may become hysterical, as shell-shock leaves some with "nerve wounds as irritable and hysterically emotional as the veriest girl."[7] But women are the "true" hysterics, their physical weaknesses exacerbated by the cultural prescriptions of femininity, the "self-sacrificing love and over-careful sympathy of mother, sister, or some other devoted relative."[8]

His cure is simple: seclusion, a carefully controlled diet, bed rest of six weeks to two months, massage, and electricity to stimulate muscles. And much of the book details the circumstances of each of these elements of the cure. All must be carefully moderated and supervised and each comes with certain attendant dangers.

For example, rest is essential. Mitchell prescribes at least six weeks of complete bed rest with only about fifteen minutes twice a day to sit up in bed. This is gradually increased so that after twelve weeks, she is confined to her bed for only three to five waking hours a day. "Even after she moves

---

[7] S. Weir Mitchell, *Fat and Blood; and How to Make Them* (Philadelphia: J. B. Lippincott, 1882), p. 30.

[8] *Fat and Blood*, p. 31.

xviii *INTRODUCTION.*

about and goes out, I insist for two months on absolute repose at least two or three hours daily."[9]

Enforced rest is not without its risks and the physician must be mindful of possible harms. "When we put patients in bed and forbid them to rise or to make use of their muscles," he writes, "we at once lessen appetite, weaken digestion in many cases, constipate the bowels, and enfeeble circulation."[10] Massage is used as a counterweight to the immobility of bed rest, prescribed to "deprive rest of its evils," stimulate the muscles and organs, and flush toxins from the skin. Electricity may also be used to stimulate the muscles of the body at rest.[11]

Perhaps some of the most extreme therapeutic claims are made for Mitchell's rather extraordinary dietetic prescriptions. He prescribes what he calls a "heavy diet," administered several times a day, to overwhelm the system with healthy proteins and carbohydrates. Vitamin and iron supplements enlarge the intake. And Mitchell claims that he has "watched again and again, with growing surprise,

---

[9] *Fat and Blood*, p. 52.
[10] *Fat and Blood*, p. 49.
[11] *Fat and Blood*, p. 53.

some listless, feeble, white-blooded creature learning by degrees to consume these large rations, and gathering under their use flesh, color, and wholesomeness of mind and body."[12]

Women are especially susceptible to neurological debilities, not only because their physical constitution is so weak, but also because "the intense persistency with which some women study and dwell upon their symptoms is often the great difficulty."[13] In other words, not only are these women feeble, they're hypochondriacs. Mitchell makes it clear that he doesn't especially enjoy treating women; indeed, he writes "every medical man of large experience knows that many of these women are to him sources of anxiety or of therapeutic despair so deep that after all time he gets to think of them as destined irredeemably to a life of imperfect health."[14]

Heavy diets or large rations are also effective for males suffering from neurasthenia. On one occasion in May 1877, Mitchell was called in to consult on the case of a 53-year-old man who was so mentally

---

[12] *Fat and Blood*, p. 83.
[13] *Fat and Blood*, p. 98.
[14] *Fat and Blood*, p. 105.

and physically tired out that he was "increasingly [feeble], absolutely unable to fulfil [sic] his usual duties. . . . There was utter prostration of nervous and muscular force; his limbs refused their support; his appetites failed; the recollection of ordinary phrases involved distinct and painful effort; sleep became unattainable, except under the influence of powerful narcotics."[15] Three months later, after a physical regime coupling massive intake of milk, malt, iron supplements, and heavy meals, he had gained more than fifteen pounds, was "strong and well, has no cough, and has ceased to be what he had been for years—a delicate man."[16]

IV.

In addition to the enormous cultural changes in gender ideologies, readers may be struck by some of the empirical changes since Mitchell wrote. In chapter 1, for example, Mitchell notes that the British have more middle-aged obesity, a "fact" he attributes to the climate and prodigious drinking of beer.

---

[15] *Fat and Blood*, p. 89.
[16] *Fat and Blood*, p. 91.

Of course, today, as cultural critics like Greg Crister point out, we are the fatter culture—by far.[17]

But perhaps even more striking may be the persistence of treatment suggestions. For example, how many of us have been treated, during a sleepless night, to television infomercials for electrical belts and gadgets that enable us to lose countless pounds through electrical stimulation of the muscles while we sit on the sofa and watch TV? How many women are addicted to "slim fast" meal plans or diets that manipulate protein and carbohydrate intake in massive doses? And how many men are these days stuffing themselves with food and chemical supplements, both legal and illegal, in order to gain weight, bulk, and muscle mass, in order to become "large" or to increase sexual potency and therefore, manhood?

In that sense, Mitchell's pronouncements may be seen as cautionary tales, reminding contemporary readers of the persistence of traditional gender ideologies and the ways these ideologies are then projected onto gendered bodies. They provide a

---

[17] Greg Crister, *Fat Land: How Americans Became the Fattest People in the World* (Boston: Houghton Mifflin, 2003).

sobering historical riposte to those faddists who think they've just discovered the nutritional, metabolic, or physical regimen that will deliver on its promise of increased energy, vitality, and productivity. And finally, they remind us that those opposed to gender equality have long employed a variety of pseudo-scientific arguments to undermine women's claims for an equal footing in the public and private spheres—and that such efforts are invariably destined to fail.

FAT AND BLOOD

DEDICATION.

TO

JOHN FORSYTH MEIGS, M.D.,

IN GRATEFUL REMEMBRANCE OF MANY ACTS OF FRIENDLY SERVICE.

S. WEIR MITCHELL.

CONTENTS.

CHAPTER I.
INTRODUCTORY 9

CHAPTER II.
FAT IN ITS CLINICAL RELATIONS 11

CHAPTER III.
SECLUSION 36

CHAPTER IV.
REST 38

CHAPTER V.
MASSAGE 53

CHAPTER VI.
ELECTRICITY 64

CHAPTER VII.
DIETETICS AND THERAPEUTICS—GENERAL RESULTS—
   CASES 73

PREFACE TO THE SECOND EDITION.

THE early call for a second edition of this little volume has satisfied me that I was right in my belief that the profession was ready to examine any promising means of treating a class of disorders which it has never found easy to deal with. As yet there has hardly been time for physicians to give their verdict on the methods I have described. I am able, however, to add cases which have been watched and treated by others, and I have made some few additions to the text.

FAT AND BLOOD:

AND

HOW TO MAKE THEM.

CHAPTER I.

INTRODUCTORY.

For some years I have been using with success, in private and in hospital practice, certain methods of renewing the vitality of feeble people by a combination of entire rest and of excessive feeding, made possible by passive exercise obtained through the steady use of massage and electricity.

The cases thus treated have been chiefly women of the class well known to every physician,—nervous women, who as a rule are thin, and lack blood. Most of them have been such as had passed through many hands and been treated in turn for gastric, spinal, or uterine troubles, but who remained at the end as at the beginning, invalids, unable to attend to the duties of life, and sources alike of discomfort to themselves and anxiety to others.

I do not wish to be thought of as putting forth anything very remarkable or original in my treatment of rest, systematic feeding, and passive exercise. All of these have been used by physicians; but, as a rule, one or more are used without the others, and the plan which I have found so valuable, of combining these means, does not seem to be generally understood. As it involves some novelty, and as I do not find it described elsewhere, I shall, I think, be doing a service to my profession by relating my experience.

In 1875 I published in "Séguin's Series of American Clinical Lectures," Vol. I. No. iv., a brief sketch of this treatment, under the heading of "Rest in the Treatment of Nervous Disease," but the scope afforded me was too brief for the details on a knowledge of which depends success in the use of rest. I have been often since reminded of this by the many letters I have received asking for explanations of the minutiæ of treatment, and this must be my apology for bringing into these pages a great many particulars which are no doubt well enough known to the more accomplished physicians.

CHAPTER II.

FAT IN ITS CLINICAL RELATIONS.

The gentlemen who have done me the honor to follow my clinical service at the Infirmary for Diseases of the Nervous System are well aware how much care is given to learn whether or not the patient is losing or has lost flesh, is by habit thin or fat. This question is one of the utmost moment in every point of view, and deserves a larger share of attention than it receives. In this hospital it is our custom to weigh our cases when they enter, and at times afterwards; but I do not think that such is a constant custom elsewhere. The mere loss of fat is probably of small moment in itself when the amount of daily food is sufficient for every-day expenditure, and when the organs are in condition to keep up the supply of fat which we require. But the steady or rapid lessening of the deposits of hydro-carbons stored away in the areolæ of the tissues is of importance, as indicating their excessive use or a failure of supply; and when this is the case it becomes our duty to learn the reasons for this striking symptom. It has also, in my view of it, a collateral value of great import, because it is almost an invariable rule that rapid thinning is accompanied with more or less anæmia, and it is rare to see a person steadily gaining fat after any pathological reduction of weight without a corresponding gain in amount and quality of blood. We too rarely reflect that the blood thins with the decrease of the tissues and enriches as they increase.

Before entering into this question further, I shall ask attention to some points connected with the normal fat of the human body; and, taking for granted, here and elsewhere, that my readers are well enough aware of the physiological value and uses of the adipose tissues, I shall continue to look at the matter chiefly from a clinical point of view.

When in any individual the weight varies rapidly or slowly, it is nearly always due, for the most part, to a change in the amount of adipose tissue stored away in the meshes of the areolar tissue. Almost any grave change for the worse in health is at once betrayed in most people by a loss of fat, and this is readily seen in the altered forms of the face, which, because it is the always visible and in outline the most irregular part of the body, shows first and most plainly the loss or gain of tissue. Fatty matter is therefore that constituent of the body which goes and comes most easily. Why there is in nearly every one a normal limit to its accumulation we cannot say. Even in health the weight of men, and still more of women, is by no means constant, but, as a rule, when we are holding our own with that share of stored-up fat which belongs to the individual we are usually in a condition of nutritive prosperity, and when after any strain or trial which has lessened weight we are slowly repairing mischief and laying by fat we are equally in a state of health. The loss of fat, especially its rapid or steady loss, nearly always goes along with conditions which impoverish the blood, and, on the other hand, the gain of fat up to a certain point seems to go hand in hand with a rise in all other essentials of health, and notably with an improvement in the color and amount of the red corpuscles.

The quantity of fat which is healthy for the individual varies with the sex, the climate, the habits, the season, the time of life, the race, and the breed. Quetelet[1] has shown that before puberty the weight of the male is for equal ages above that of the female, but that towards puberty the proportional weight of the female, due chiefly to gain in fat, in-

---

[1] Sur l'Homme, p. 47, et seq.

creases, so that at twelve the two sexes are alike in this respect. During the child-bearing time there is an absolute diminution on the part of the female, but after this time the weight of the woman increases and the maximum is attained at about the age of fifty.

Dr. Henry I. Bowditch[1] reaches somewhat similar conclusions, and shows from much more numerous measurements of Boston children that growing boys are heavier in proportion to their height than girls until they reach fifty-eight inches, which is attained about the fourteenth year. Then the girl passes the boy in weight, which Dr. Bowditch thinks is due to the accumulation of adipose tissue at puberty. After two or three years more the male again acquires and retains superiority in weight and height.

Yet during life there are peculiarities which belong to individuals and to families. One group thins as life goes on past forty; another group as surely takes on flesh; and the same traits are often inherited, and are to be regarded when the question of fattening becomes of clinical or diagnostic moment. Men, as a rule, preserve their nutritive status more equably than women. Every physician must have been struck with this. In fact, many women lose or ac-

---

[1] Growth of Children, p. 31.

quire large amounts of adipose matter without any corresponding loss or gain in vigor, and this fact perhaps is related in some way to the enormous outside demands made by her peculiar physiological processes. Such gain in weight is a common accompaniment of child-bearing, while nursing in some involves enormous falling away, and its cessation a renewal of fat as speedy. I have also found that in many women who are not perfectly well there is a notable loss of weight at every menstrual period, and a marked gain between these times.

How much influence the season has, is not as yet well understood, but in our own climate, with its great extremes, there are some interesting facts in this connection. The wealthy classes are with us in summer placed in the best circumstances for increase in flesh, because it is not only their season of least work, mental and physical, but because they are then for the most part living in the country under circumstances favorable to appetite and to exercise. Owing to these fortunate conditions members of the class in question are apt to gain weight in summer, although many persons, as I know, follow the general rule and lose weight. But if we deal with the mass of men who are hard worked, physically, and unable to leave the towns, we shall probably find that they nearly always lose weight in hot weather. Some support is given to this idea by the following very curious facts. Many years ago I was engaged for certain purposes in determining the weight, height, and girth of all the members of our city police force. The examination was made in April and repeated in the beginning of October. Every care was taken to avoid errors, but to my surprise I found that a large majority of the men had lost weight during the summer. The sum total of loss was enormous. As I have mislaid some of the sheets I am unable to give it accurately, but I found that three out of every five had lessened in weight. It would be interesting to know if such a change occurs in convicts confined in penitentiaries.

I am acquainted with some persons who lose weight in winter, and with more who fail in flesh in the spring, which is our season of greatest depression in health—the season when choreas are apt to originate[1] or to recur, and when habitual epileptic fits become frequent in such as are the victims of that disease.

Climate has a good deal to do with a tendency to take on fat, and I think the first thing which strikes

---

[1] See a valuable paper by Dr. Gerhard. Am. Journ. Med. Sci., 1876.

an American in England is the number of inordinately fat middle-aged people, and especially of fat women.

This excess of flesh we usually associate in idea with slothfulness, but English women exercise more than ours, and live in a land where few days forbid it, so that probably such a tendency to obesity is due chiefly to climatic causes. To this also we may no doubt ascribe the habits of the English as to food. They are larger feeders than we, and both sexes consume beer in a manner which would in this country be destructive of health. These habits aid, I suspect, in producing the more general fatness in middle and later life, and those enormous occasional growths which so amaze an American when first he sets foot in London. But whatever be the cause, it is probable that of the prosperous classes English, over forty, would outweigh the average American of that period, and this must make, I should think, some difference in their relative liability to certain forms of disease, because the overweight of our transAtlantic cousins is plainly due to excess of fat.

I have sought in vain for English tables giving the weight of men and women of various heights at like ages. The material for such a study of men in America is given in Gould's researches, United

States Sanitary Commission, and in Baxter's admirable report, but is lacking for women. A comparison of these points as between English and Americans of both sexes, would be of great interest.

I doubt whether, in this country, as great a growth as multitudes of English attain be either healthy or desirable in point of comfort, owing to the distress which stout people feel in our hot summer weather. Certainly "Banting" is with us a rarely-needed process, and, as a rule, we have much more frequent occasion to fatten than to thin our patients. The climatic peculiarities which have changed our voices, sharpened our features, and made small the American hand and foot, have also made us, in middle and advanced life, a thinner and more sallow race, and, possibly, adapted us better to the region in which we live. The same changes in form are in like manner showing themselves in the English race in Australia.[1]

---

[1] This excess of corpulence in the English is attained chiefly after forty, as I have said. The average American is taller than the average Englishman, and is fully as well built in proportion to his height, as Gould has shown. The child of either sex in New England is both taller and heavier than the English child of corresponding class and age, as Dr. H. I. Bowditch has lately made clear; while the English of the manufacturing and agricultural classes are miserably inferior to the members of a similar class in America.

Some gain in flesh as life goes on is a frequent thing here as elsewhere, and usually has no unwholesome meaning. Occasionally we see people past the age of sixty suddenly taking on fat and becoming at once unwieldy and feeble, the fat collecting in masses about the belly and around the joints. Such an increase is usually accompanied with fatty degeneration of the heart and muscles, and with a certain watery flabbiness in the limbs, which, however, do not pit on pressure.

Alcoholism also gives rise in some people to a vast increase of adipose tissue, and the sodden, unwholesome fatness of the hard drinker is a sufficiently well-known and unpleasant spectacle. The overgrowth of inert people who do not exercise enough to use up a healthy amount of over-fed tissues is common enough as an individual peculiarity, but there are also two other conditions in which fat is apt to be accumulated to an uncomfortable extent. Thus, in some cases of hysteria where the patient lies abed from belief that she is unable to move about, she is apt in time to become enormously stout. This seems to me also to be favored by the large use of morphia to which such women are prone, so that I should say that long rest, the hysterical constitution, and the accompanying resort to morphia made up a group of factors highly favorable to increase of fat.

Lastly, there is the class of fat anæmic people, usually women. This double condition is not very uncommon, but as the mass of thin-blooded persons are as a rule thin or losing flesh, there must be some peculiarity in that anæmia which goes with gain in flesh.

Bauer[1] thinks that lessened number of blood-corpuscles gives rise to storing of fat, owing to lessened tissue-combustion. At all events the absorbed oxygen diminishes after bleeding, and it used to be well known that some people grew fat when bled at intervals. Also, it is said that cattle-breeders in some localities—certainly not in this country—bleed their cattle to cause increase of fat in the tissues, or of fat secreted as butter in the milk. These explanations aid us but little to comprehend what after all is only met with in certain persons, and must therefore involve factors not common to every one who is anæmic. Meanwhile, the group of fat anæmics is of the utmost clinical interest, as I shall by and by point out more distinctly.

---

[1] Zeitschrift für Biol., 1872. Phil. Med. Times, vol. iii. page 115.

There is a popular idea, which has probably passed from the agriculturist into the common mind of the community, to the effect that human fat varies,— that some fat is wholesome and some unwholesome, that there are good fats and bad fats. I remember well an old nurse who assured me when I was a student that "some fats is fast and some is fickle, but cod-oil fat is easy squandered."

There are more facts in favor of some such idea than I have place for, but as yet we have no distinct chemical knowledge as to whether the fats put on under alcohol or morphia, or rapidly by the use of oils, or pathologically in fatty degenerations, or in anæmia, vary in their constituents. It is not at all unlikely that such is the case, and that, for example, the fat of an obese anæmic person may differ from that of a fat and florid person.

The flabby, relaxed state of many fat people is possibly due not alone to peculiarities of the fat but also to want of tone and tension in the areolar tissues, which, from all that we now know of them, may be capable of undergoing changes as marked as those of muscles.

That, however, animals may take on fat which varies in character is well known to breeders of cattle. "The art of breeding and feeding stock," says Dr.

Letheby,[1] "is to overcome excessive tendency to accumulation of either surface fat or visceral fat, and at the same time to produce a fat which will not melt or boil away in cooking. Oily foods have a tendency to make soft fats which will not bear cooking." Such differences are also seen between English and American bacon, the former being much more solid; and we know, also, that the fat of different animals varies remarkably, and that some, as the fat of hay-fed horses, is readily worked off. Such facts as these may reasonably be held to sustain the popular creed as to there being bad fats and good fats, and they teach us the lesson that in man as in animals there may be a difference in the value of the fats we acquire, according as they are gained by one means or by another.

I have had occasion, of late years, to watch with interest the process of somewhat rapid but quite wholesome gain in flesh in persons subjected to the treatment which I shall by and by describe. Most of these persons were treated by massage, and I have been accustomed to question the masseur or masseuse as to the manner in which the change takes place. Usually it is first seen in the face and neck, then it

---

[1] Letheby on Food, pp. 39, 40, 44.

FAT IN ITS CLINICAL RELATIONS. 23

is noticed in the back and flanks, next in the belly, and finally in the limbs, the legs coming last in the order of gain, and sometimes remaining comparatively thin long after other parts have made remarkable and visible gain. These observations have been checked by careful measurements, so that I am sure of their correctness for people who fatten while at rest in bed. The order of increase might be different in people who fatten while afoot.

Looking back over the whole subject, it will be well for the physician to remember that increase of fat, to be a wholesome condition, should be accompanied by gain in quantity and quality of blood, and that while increase of flesh after illness is desirable, and a good test of successful recovery, it should always go along with improvement in color. Obesity with thin blood is one of the most unmanageable conditions I know of.

The exact relations of fatty tissue to the condition of health are not as yet well understood; but, since on great exertion or prolonged mental or moral strain or in low fevers we lose fat rapidly, it may be taken for granted that each individual should possess a certain surplus of this readily-lost material. It is the one portion of our body which comes and goes in large amount. Even thin people have it in some quantity always ready, and, despite the fluctuations, every one has a standard share, which varies at different times of life. The mechanism which limits the storing away of an excess is almost unknown, and we are only aware that some foods and lack of exertion favor growth in fat, while action and lessened diet diminish it; but also we know that while any one can be made to lose weight, there are some persons who cannot be made to gain a pound by any possible device, so that in this, as in other things, to spend is easier than to get; although it is clear that the very thin must certainly live, so to speak, from hand to mouth, and have little for emergencies. Whether fat people possess greater power of resistance, as against the fatal wasting of certain maladies or not, does not seem to be known, and I fancy that the popular medical belief is rather opposed to the vital endurance of those who are unusually fat.

At present, however, we have to do most largely with the means of attaining that moderate share of stored-away fat which seems to indicate a state of nutritive prosperity and to be essential to those physical needs, such as protection and padding, which fat subserves no less than to its æsthetic value, as rounding the curves of the human form.

The study of the amount of the different forms of

diet which are needed by people at rest, and by those who are active, is valuable only to enable us to construct dietaries with care for masses of men and where economy is an object. In dealing with cases such as I shall describe it is needful usually to give and have digested an overplus of food, so that we are more concerned now to know the forms of food which thin or fatten, and the means which aid us to digest temporarily an excess.

As to quantity, it suffices to say that while by lessening food we may easily and surely make people lose weight, we cannot be sure to fatten by merely increasing the amount of food given; something more is wanted in the way of digestives or tonics to enable the patient to prepare and appropriate what is given, and but too often we fail miserably in all our means of giving capacity to assimilate food. As I have said before and wish to repeat, to gain in fat is nearly always to gain in blood; and I hope to point out in these pages some of the means by which these ends can be attained when all usual methods have failed.

There are, of course, a multitude of cases in which it becomes desirable to fatten and to make blood, but in many of them these are easy tasks, and in some altogether hopeless. Persons who are recovering healthfully from fevers, pneumonias, and other temporary maladies, gather flesh and make blood readily, and we need only to help them by the ordinary tonics, careful feeding, and change of air in due season.

In other and fatal or graver maladies, in such cases, for example, as pulmonary phthisis, however proper it may be to fatten, it is almost an impossible task, and, as Pollock remarks, the lung-trouble may be advancing even while the patient is gaining in weight.

There remains a class of cases desirable to fatten and redden which are often, or usually, chronic in character, and present among them some of the most difficult problems which perplex the physician. If I pause to dwell upon these, it is because they are the forms of disease in which my plan of treatment has had the largest success; it is because some of them are simply living records of the failure of every other rational and many irrational plans; it is because many of them find no place in the text-book, however sadly familiar they are to the physician.

The group I would speak of contains that large number of people who are kept meagre and often also anæmic by constant dyspepsia, in its varied forms, or by those defects in assimilative processes which, while more obscure, are as fertile parents of similar mischiefs. Let me add the long-continued malarial poisonings, and we have a group of varied origin which is a moderate percentage of cases in which loss of weight and of color are noticeable, and in which the usual therapeutic methods do sometimes utterly fail.

For many of these, fresh air, exercise, change of scene, tonics, and stimulants are alike valueless; and for them the concentration of tonic influences I shall describe, when used with absolute rest, massage, and electricity, are often of inestimable service.

A portion of the last class I referred to above, and which I have yet to describe, is one I have hinted at as the despair of the physician. It includes that large group of women, especially, said to have nervous exhaustion, or who are described as having spinal irritation, if that be the prominent symptom. To it I must add cases in which, besides the wasting and anæmia, emotional manifestations predominate, and which are then called hysterical, whether or not they exhibit ovarian or uterine disorders.

Nothing is more common in practice than to see a young woman who falls below the health-standard, loses color and plumpness, is tired all the time, by and by has a tender spine, and soon or late enacts the whole varied drama of hysteria. As one or other set of symptoms is prominent she gets the appropriate label, and sometimes she continues to exhibit only the single phase of nervous exhaustion or of spinal irritation. Far more often she runs the gauntlet of nerve-doctors, gynæcologists, plaster-jackets, braces, water-treatment, and all the fantastic variety of other cures.

It will be worth while to linger here a little and more sharply delineate the classes of cases I have just named.

I see every week—almost every day—women who when asked what is the matter reply, "Oh, I have nervous exhaustion." When further questioned, they answer that everything tires them. Now, it is vain to speak of all of these cases as hysterical, or, as Paget has done, as mimetic. It is quite sure that in the graver examples exercise quickens the pulse curiously, the tire shows in the face, or sometimes diarrhœa or nausea follows exertion, and though while under excitement or in the presence of some dominant motive they can do a good deal, the exhaustion which ensues is in proportion to the exercise used.

I have rarely seen such a case which was not more

or less lacking in color and which had not lost flesh; the exceptions being those troublesome cases of fat anæmic people which I shall by and by speak of more fully.

Perhaps a full sketch of one of these cases will be better than any list of symptoms: A woman, most often between twenty and thirty, undergoes a season of trial or encounters some prolonged strain. She undertakes the hard task of nursing a relative, and goes through this severe duty with the addition of emotional excitement, swayed by hopes and fears, and forgetful of self and of what every one needs in the way of air and food and change when attempting this most trying task; or possibly it is mere physical strain, such as teaching. In another set of cases an illness is the cause, and she never rallies entirely, or else some local uterine trouble starts the mischief, and although this is cured the doctor wonders that his patient does not get fat and ruddy again.

But no matter how it comes about, the woman grows pale and thin, eats little, or if she eats does not profit by it. Everything wearies her,—to sew, to write, to read, to walk,—and by and by the sofa or the bed is her only comfort. Every effort is paid for dearly, and she describes herself as aching and sore, as sleeping ill, and as needing constant stimulus and endless tonics. Then comes the mischievous rôle of bromides, opium, chloral, and brandy. If the case did not begin with uterine troubles they soon appear, and are usually treated in vain if the general means employed to build up the bodily health fail, as in many of these cases they do fail. The same remark applies to the dyspepsias and constipation which further annoy the patient and embarrass the treatment. If such a person is emotional she does not fail to become more so, and even the firmest women lose self-control at last under incessant feebleness. Nor is this less true of men, and I have many a time seen soldiers who had ridden boldly with Sheridan or fought gallantly with Grant become, under the influence of painful nerve-wounds, as irritable and hysterically emotional as the veriest girl. If no rescue comes, the fate of women thus disordered is at last the bed. They acquire tender spines, and furnish the most lamentable examples of all the strange phenomena of hysteria.

The moral degradation which such cases undergo is pitiable. I have heard a good deal of the disciplinary usefulness of sickness, and this may apply to brief, and what I might call wholesome, maladies. I have seen a few people who were ennobled by long sickness, but far more often the result is to cultivate self-love and selfishness and to take away by slow degrees the healthy mastery which every human being should retain over her own emotions and wants.

There is one fatal addition to the weight which tends to destroy women who suffer in the way I have described. It is the self-sacrificing love and over-careful sympathy of a mother, a sister, or some other devoted relative. Nothing is more curious, nothing more sad and pitiful, than these partnerships between the sick and selfish and the sound and over-loving. By slow but sure degrees the healthy life is absorbed by the sick life, in a manner more or less injurious to both, until, sometimes too late for remedy, the growth of the evil is seen by others. Usually the person withdrawn from wholesome duties to minister to the caprices of hysterical sensitiveness is the person of a household who feels most for the invalid, and who for this very reason suffers the most. The patient has pain, a tender spine, for example; she is urged to give it rest. She cannot read; the self-constituted nurse reads to her. At last light hurts her eyes; the mother remains shut up with her all day in a darkened room. A draught of air is supposed to do harm, and the doors and windows are closed, and the ingenuity of kindness is taxed to imagine new sources of like trouble, until at last the window-cracks are stuffed with cotton, the chimney stopped, and even the keyhole guarded. It is easy to see where this all leads to,—the nurse falls ill, and a new victim is found. I have seen a hysterical, anæmic girl kill in this way three generations of nurses. If you tell the patient she is basely selfish she is probably amazed, and wonders at your cruelty. To cure such a case you must morally alter as well as physically amend, and nothing less will answer. The first step needful is to break up the companionship, and to substitute the firm kindness of a well-trained hired nurse.[1]

Another form of evil to be encountered in these cases is less easy to deal with. Such an invalid has by unhappy chance to live with some near relative whose temperament is also nervous and who is impatient or irritable. Two such people produce endless mischief for one another. In other examples there is a strange incompatibility which it is difficult to define. The two people who, owing to their relationship, depend the one on the other, are for no good reason made unhappy by their several

---

[1] "Nurse and Patient," S. Weir Mitchell, Lippincott's Magazine, Dec. 1872.

peculiarities. Life-long annoyance results, and for them there is no divorce possible.

In a smaller number of cases, which have less tendency to emotional disturbances, the phenomena are more simple. You have to deal with a woman who has lost flesh and grown colorless, but has no hysterical tendencies. She is merely a person hopelessly below the standard of health and subject to a host of aches and pains, without notable organic disease. Why such people should sometimes be so hard to cure I cannot say. But the sad fact remains. Iron, acids, travel, water-cures have for a certain proportion of them no value, or little value, and they remain for years feeble and forever tired. For them, as for the whole class, the pleasures of life are limited by this perpetual weariness and by the asthenopia which they rarely escape, and which, by preventing them from reading, leaves them free to study day after day their accumulating aches and distresses.

Medical opinion must, of course, vary as to the causes which give rise to the familiar cases I have so briefly sketched. In fact they vary endlessly; but I imagine that few physicians placed face to face with such cases would not feel sure that if they could give the patient a liberal gain in fat and in blood they would be certain to need very little else, and that the troubles of stomach, bowels and uterus would speedily vanish. Such has certainly been the result of my own very ample experience. If I succeed in first altering the moral atmosphere which has been to the patient like the very breathing of evil, and if I can add largely to the weight and fill the vessels with red blood, I am usually sure of giving relief. If I fail it is because I fail in these very points, or else because I have overlooked or undervalued some serious organic tissue-change.

If I did not know that I had been happy in thus aiding numberless cases in which others had failed, I should not have ventured to write these pages; and if I have succeeded it must be because the methods pursued have been other than those now commonly in use.

In the following chapters I shall treat of the means which I have employed, and shall not hesitate to give such minute details as shall enable others to profit by my failures and successes. In describing the remedies used, and the mode of using them in combination, I shall relate a sufficient number of cases to illustrate both the happier results and the causes of occasional failure.

The treatment I am about to describe consists in

seclusion, certain forms of diet, rest in bed, massage (or manipulation), and electricity; and I desire to insist anew on the fact that it is the use of these means together that is wanted. The necessities of my subject will of course oblige me to treat of each of them in a separate chapter.

CHAPTER III.

SECLUSION.

It is rare to find any of the class of patients I have described so free from the influence of their habitual surroundings as to make it easy to treat them in their own homes. It is needful to disentangle them from the meshes of old habits and to remove them from the contact with those who have been the willing slaves of their caprices. I have often made the effort to treat them in their own homes and to isolate them there, but I have rarely done so without promising myself that I would not again complicate my treatment by any such embarrassments. Once separate the patient from the moral and physical surroundings which have become part of her life of sickness, and you will have made a change which will be in itself beneficial, and will enormously aid in the treatment which is to follow. Of course this step is not essential in such cases as are merely anæmic and feeble and thin, owing to distinct causes, like the exhaustion of overwork and of long dyspepsia; but I am now speaking chiefly of the large and troublesome class of thin-blooded emotional women, for whom a state of weak health has become a long and almost, I might say, a cherished habit. For them there is often no success possible until we have broken up the whole daily drama of the sick-room, with its little selfishnesses and its craving for sympathy and indulgence. Nor should we hesitate to insist upon this change, for not only shall we then act in the true interests of the patient, but we shall also confer on those near to her an inestimable benefit. A hysterical girl is, as Wendell Holmes has said in his decisive phrase, a vampire who sucks the blood of the healthy people about her; and I may add that pretty surely where there is one hysterical girl there will be soon or late two sick women.

I should add here a few words of caution as to the time of year best fitted for treatment. In the summer seclusion is often undesirable when the patient is well enough to gain help by change of air; moreover, at this season massage is less agreeable than in winter, and, as a rule, I find it harder to feed and to fatten persons at rest during our summer heats. That this rule is not without exception is shown by a case which I have quoted in the final chapter.

CHAPTER IV.

REST.

I HAVE said more than once in the early chapters of this little volume that the treatment I wished to advise as of use in a certain range of cases was made up of rest, massage, electricity, and over-feeding. I said that the use of large amounts of food while at rest, more or less entire, was made possible by the practice of kneading the muscles and by moving them with currents able to effect this end. I desire now to discuss in turn the mode in which I employ rest, massage, and electricity, and, as I have promised, I shall take pains to give, in regard to these three subjects, the fullest details, because success in the treatment depends, I am sure, on the care with which we look after a number of things each in itself of slight moment.

I have no doubt that many doctors have seen fit at times to put their patients at rest for great or small lengths of time, but the person who of all others within my knowledge used this means most, and used it so as to obtain the best results, was the late Professor Samuel Jackson. He was in the habit of making his patients remain in bed for many weeks at a time, and, if I recall his cases well, he used this treatment in just the class of disorders among women which have given me the best results. What these are I have been at some pains to define, and I have now only to show why in such people rest is of service, and what I mean by rest, and how I apply it.

In No. IV. of Dr. Séguin's series of American Clinical Lectures, I was at some pains to point out the value of repose in neuralgias, in myelitis, and in the early stages of locomotor ataxia. I shall now confine myself chiefly to its use in the various forms of weakness which exist with thin blood and wasting, with or without distinct lesions of the stomach or womb.

Whether we shall ask a patient to walk or to take rest is a question which turns up for answer almost every day in practice. Most often we incline to insist on exercise, and are led to do so from a belief that women walk too little, and that to move about a good deal every day is good for everybody. I think we are as often wrong as right. A good brisk daily walk is for well folks a tonic, breaks down old tissues, and creates a wholesome demand for food. The same is true for some sick people. The habit of horse exercise or a long walk every day is needed to cure or to aid in the cure of disordered stomach and costive bowels, but if all exertion gives rise only to increase of trouble, to extreme sense of fatigue, to nausea, what shall we do? And suppose that tonics do not help to make exertion easy, and that the great tonic of change of air fails us, shall we still persist? And here lies the trouble: there are women who mimic fatigue, who indulge themselves in rest on the least pretence, who have no symptoms so truly honest that we need care to regard them. These are they who spoil their own nervous systems as they spoil their children, when they have them, by yielding to the least desire and teaching them to dwell on little pains. For such people there is no help but to insist on self-control and on daily use of the limbs. They must be told to exert themselves, and made to do so if that can be. If they are young this is easy enough. If they have grown to middle life, and made long habits of self-indulgence, the struggle is always useless. But few, however, among these women are free from some defect of blood or tissue, either original or having come on as a result of years of indolence and attention to aches and ailments which should never have had given to them more than a passing thought, and which certainly should not have been made an excuse for the sofa or the bed.

Sometimes the question is easy to settle. If you find a woman who is in good state as to color and flesh, and who is always able to do what it pleases her to do, and who is tired by what does not please her, that is a woman to order out of bed and to control with a firm and steady will. That is a woman who is to be made to walk, with no regard to her aches, and to be made to persist until exertion ceases to give rise to the mimicry of fatigue. In such cases the man who can insure belief in his opinions and obedience to his decrees secures very often most brilliant and sometimes easy success; and it is in such cases that women who are in all other ways capable doctors fail, because they do not obtain the needed control over those of their own sex. There are still other cases in which the same mischievous tendencies to repose, to endless tire, to hysterical symptoms, and to emotional displays have grown out of defects of nutrition so distinct that no man ought to think for them of mere exertion as a sole means of cure. The time comes for that, but it should not come until entire rest has been used, with other means, to fit them for making use of their muscles. Nothing upsets these cases like over-exertion, and the attempt to make them walk usually ends in some mischievous emotional display, and in creating a new reason for thinking that they cannot walk. As to the two sets of cases just sketched, no one need hesitate; the one must walk, the other should not until we have bettered her nutritive state. She may be able to drag herself about, but no good will be done by making her do so. But between these two classes lies the larger number of such cases, giving us every kind of real and imagined symptom, and dreadfully well fitted to puzzle the most competent physician. As a rule, no harm is done by rest, even in such people as give us doubts about whether it is or is not well for them to exert themselves. There are plenty of these women who are just well enough to make it likely that if they had motive enough for exertion to cause them to forget themselves they would find it useful. In the doubt I am rather given to insisting on rest, but the rest I like for them is not at all their notion of rest. To lie abed half the day, and sew a little and read a little, and be interesting and excite sympathy, is all very well, but when they are bidden to stay in bed a month, and neither to read, write, nor sew, and to have one nurse,—who is not a relative, —then rest becomes for some women a rather bitter medicine, and they are glad enough to accept the order to rise and go about when the doctor issues a mandate which has become pleasantly welcome and eagerly looked for. I do not think it easy to make a mistake in this matter unless the woman takes with morbid delight to the system of enforced rest, and unless the doctor is a person of feeble will. I have never met myself with any serious trouble about getting out of bed any woman for whom I thought rest needful, but it has happened to others, and the man who resolves to send any nervous woman to bed must be quite sure that she will obey him when the time comes for her to get up.

I have, of course, made use of every grade of rest for my patients, from insisting upon repose on a lounge for some hours a day up to entire rest in bed. In carrying out my general plan of treatment it is my habit to ask the patient to remain in bed from six weeks to two months. At first, and in some cases for four or five weeks, I do not permit the patient to sit up or to sew or write or read. The only action allowed is that needed to clean the teeth. In some instances I have not permitted the patient to turn over without aid, and this I have done because sometimes I think no motion desirable, and because sometimes the moral influence of absolute repose is of use. In such cases I arrange to have the bowels and water passed while lying down, and the patient is lifted on to a lounge at bedtime and sponged, and then lifted back again into the newly-made bed. In all cases of weakness, treated by rest, I insist on the patient being fed by the nurse, and, when well enough to sit up in bed, I insist that the meats shall be cut up, so as to make it easier for the patient to feed herself.

In many cases I allow the patient to sit up in order to obey the calls of nature, but I am always careful to have the bowels kept reasonably free from costiveness, knowing well how such a state and the efforts it gives rise to enfeeble a sick person.

Usually, after a fortnight I permit the patient to be read to,—one to three hours a day,—but I am daily amazed to see how kindly nervous and anæmic women take to this absolute rest, and how little they complain of its monotony. In fact, the use of massage and the battery, with the frequent comings of the nurse with food and the doctor's visits, seem so to fill up the day as to make the treatment less tiresome than might be supposed. And, besides this, the sense of comfort which is apt to come about the fifth or sixth day,—the feeling of ease, and the ready capacity to digest food, and the growing hope of final cure, fed as it is by present relief,—all conspire to make most patients contented and tractable.

The moral uses of enforced rest are readily estimated. From a restless life of irregular hours, and probably endless drugging, from hurtful sympathy and over-zealous care, the patient passes to an atmosphere of quiet, to order and control, to the system and care of a thorough nurse, to an absence of drugs, and to simple diet. The result is always at first, whatever it may be afterwards, a sense of relief, and a remarkable and often a quite abrupt disappearance of many of the nervous symptoms with which we are all of us only too sadly familiar.

All the moral uses of rest and isolation and change of habits are not obtained by merely insisting on the physical conditions needed to effect these ends. If the physician has the force of character required to secure the confidence and respect of his patients he has also much more in his power, and should have the tact to seize the proper occasions to direct the thoughts of his patients to the lapse from duties to others, and to the selfishness which a life of invalidism is apt to bring about. Such moral medication belongs to the higher sphere of the doctor's duties, and if he means to cure his patient permanently, he cannot afford to neglect them. Above all, let him be careful that the masseuse and the nurse do not talk of the patient's ills, and let him by degrees teach the sick person how very essential it is to speak of her aches and pains to no one but himself.

I have often asked myself why rest is of value in the cases of which I am now speaking, and I have already alluded briefly to some of the modes in which it is of use.

Let us take first the simpler cases. We meet now and then with feeble people who are dyspeptic, and who find that exercise after a meal, or indeed much exercise on any day, is sure to cause loss of power or lessened power to digest food. The same thing is seen in an extreme degree in the well-known experiment of causing a dog to run violently after eating, in which case digestion is entirely suspended. Whether these results be due to the calling off of blood from the gastric organs to the muscles, or whether the nervous system is, for some reason, unable to evolve at the same time the force needed for a double purpose, is not quite clear, but the fact is undoubted, and finds added illustrations in many of the class of exhausted women. It is plain that this trouble exists in some of them. It is likely that it is present in a larger number. The use of rest in these people admits of no question. If we are to give them the means in blood and flesh of carrying on the work of life, it must be done with the aid of the stomach, and we must humor that organ until it is able to act in a more healthy manner under ordinary conditions.

The muscular system in many of such patients—I mean in ever-weary, thin, and thin-blooded persons—is doing its work with constant difficulty. As a result, fatigue comes early, is extreme, and lasts long. The demand for nutritive aid is ahead of the supply, and before the tissues are rebuilded a new demand is made, so that the materials of disintegration accumulate, and do this the more easily because the eliminative organs share in the general defects. And these are some of the reasons why anæmic people are always tired; but, besides this, all real sensations are magnified by women whose nervous systems have become sensitive owing to a life of attention to their ailments, and so at last it becomes hard to separate the true from the false, and we are thus led to be too skeptical as to the presence of real causes of annoyance. Certain it is that rest, under proper conditions, is found by such sufferers to be a great relief; but rest alone will not answer, and it is needful, as I shall show, to bring to our help certain other means, in order to secure all the good which repose may be made to insure.

In dealing with this, as with every other medical means, it is well to recall that in our attempts to help we may sometimes do harm, and we must make sure that in causing the largest share of good we do the least possible evil.

" The one goes with the other, as shadow with light, and to no therapeutic measure does this apply more surely than to the use of rest.

" Let us take the simplest case,—that which arises daily in the treatment of joint-troubles or broken bones. We put the limb in splints, and thus, for a time, check its power to move. The bone knits, or the joint gets well; but the muscles waste, the skin dries, the nails may for a time cease to grow, nutrition is brought down, as an arithmetician would say, to its lowest terms, and when the bone or joint is well we have a limb which is in a state of disease. As concerns broken bones, the evil may be slight and easy of relief, if the surgeon will but remember that when joints are put at rest too long they soon fall a prey to a form of arthritis, which is the more apt to be severe the older the patient is, and may be easily avoided by frequent motion of the joints, which, to be healthful, exact a certain share of daily movement. If, indeed, with perfect stillness of the fragments we could have the full life of a limb in action,

I suspect that the cure of the break might be far more rapid.

"What is true of the part is true of the whole. When we put the entire body at rest we create certain evils while doing some share of good, and it is therefore our part to use such means as shall, in every case, lessen and limit the ills we cannot wholly avoid. How to reach these ends I shall by and by state, but for a brief space I should like to dwell on some of the bad results which come of our efforts to reach through rest in bed all the good which it can give us, and to these points I ask the most thoughtful attention, because upon the care with which we meet and provide for them depends the value which we will get out of this most potent means of treatment.

"When we put patients in bed and forbid them to rise or to make use of their muscles, we at once lessen appetite, weaken digestion in many cases, constipate the bowels, and enfeeble circulation."[1]

When we put the muscles at absolute rest we create certain difficulties, because the normal acts of repeated movement insure a certain rate of nutrition which brings blood to the active parts, and without which the currents flow more largely around than through the muscles. The lessened blood-supply is

---

[1] Lecture, op. cit.

a result of diminished functional movement, and we need to create a constant demand in the inactive parts. But, besides this, every active muscle is practically a throbbing heart, squeezing its vessels empty while in motion, and relaxing, so as to allow them to fill up anew. Thus, both for itself and in its relations to the rest of the body, its activity is functionally of service. Then, also, the vessels, unaided by changes of posture and by motion, lose tone, and the distant local circuits, for all of these reasons, cease to receive their normal supply, so that defects of nutrition occur, and, with these, defects of temperature.

"I was struck with the extent to which these evils may go, in the case of Mrs. P., æt. 52, who was brought to the Infirmary from New Jersey, having been supine in bed fifteen years. I soon knew that she was free of disease, and had stayed in bed at first because there was some lack of power and much pain on rising, and at last because she had the firm belief that she could not walk. After a week's massage I made her get up. I had won her full trust, and she obeyed, or tried to obey me, like a child. But she would faint and grow deadly pale, even if seated a short time. The heart-beats rose from sixty to one hundred and thirty, and grew feeble; the breath came fast, and she had to lie down at once. Her skin was dry, sallow, and bloodless, her muscles flabby; and when, at last, after a fortnight more, I set her on her feet again, she had to endure for a time the most dreadful vertigo and alarming palpitations of the heart, while her feet, in a few minutes of feeble walking, would swell so as to present the most strange appearance. By and by all this went away, and in a month she could walk, sit up, sew, read, and, in a word, live like others. She went home a well-cured woman.

"Let us think, then, when we put a person in bed, that we are lessening the heart-beats some twenty a minute, nearly a third; that we are making the tardy blood to linger in the by-ways of the blood-round, for it has its by-ways; that rest prone binds the bowels, and tends to destroy the desire to eat; and that muscles in rest too long get to be unhealthy and shrunken in substance. Bear these ills in mind, and be ready to meet them, and we shall have answered the hard question of how to help by rest without hurt to the patient."[1]

When I first made use of this treatment I allowed my patients to get up too suddenly, and in some cases I thus brought on relapses and a return of the

---

[1] Lecture, op. cit. In the July number (1876) of the Chicago *Journal of Mental and Nervous Disease* is an able review of my lecture, in which are some criticisms which I accept as correct, and which I have used to improve my statements of the causes of some of the evils of rest.

feeling of painful fatigue. I also saw in some of these cases what I still see at times,—a rapid loss of flesh.

I now begin by permitting the patient to sit up in bed, then to feed herself, and next to sit up out of bed a few minutes at bedtime. In a week, she is desired to sit up fifteen minutes twice a day, and this is gradually increased until, at the end of twelve weeks, she rests on the bed only three to five hours daily. Even after she moves about and goes out, I insist for two months on absolute repose at least two or three hours daily.

CHAPTER V.

MASSAGE.

How to deprive rest of its evils is the subject with which I might very well have labelled this chapter. I have pointed out what I mean by rest, how it hurts, and how it seems to help; and as I believe that it is useful in most cases only if employed in conjunction with other means, the study of these becomes of the first importance.

The two aids which by degrees I learned to call upon with confidence to enable me to use rest without doing harm are massage and electricity. We have first to deal with massage, and I willingly give to it a chapter of careful detail, because as yet it is little understood in America, and because I have some facts to relate in regard to it which are not known, I think, on either side of the Atlantic.

It is many years since I first saw in this city systematic massage used by a charlatan in a case of progressive paralysis. The temporary results he obtained were so remarkable that I began soon after to learn what I could of its employment and to train some of the nurses I had in charge of cases to make use of it. Somewhat later I employed it in the earlier cases which I treated by rest, and I very soon found that I had in it an agent little understood and of singular utility.

It will be necessary, in pursuance of my plan, to describe exactly how this means is employed and why it is employed.

I can better speak of what it does after carefully specifying the manner of its use.

After a few days of the milk diet, with which my treatment ordinarily begins, the masseur or masseuse is set to work. An hour is chosen midway between two meals, and, the patient lying in bed, the manipulator starts at the feet and gently but firmly pinches up the skin, rolling it lightly between his fingers and going carefully over the whole foot; then the toes are bent and moved about in every direction, and next with the thumbs and fingers the little muscles of the foot are kneaded and pinched more largely, and the inter-osseous groups worked at with the finger-tips between the bones. At last the whole tissues of the foot are seized with both hands and somewhat firmly rolled about. Next the ankles are dealt with in like fashion, all the crevices between the articulating bones being sought out and kneaded, while the joint is put in every possible position. The leg is next treated, first by surface-pinching, and then by deeper grasping of the areolar tissue, and last by industrious and deeper pinching of the large muscular masses, which for this purpose are put in a position of the utmost relaxation. The grasp of the muscles is momentary, and for the large muscles of the calf and thigh both hands act, the one contracting as the other loosens its grip. In treating the firm muscles in front of the leg, the fingers are made to roll the muscle under the cushions of the finger-tips. At brief intervals the manipulator seizes the limb in both hands and lightly runs the grasp upwards, so as to favor the flow of venous blood-currents, and then returns to the kneading of the muscles.

The same process is carried on in every part of the body, and especial care is given to the muscles of the loins and spine, while usually the face is not touched. The belly is first treated by pinching the skin, then by deeply grasping and rolling the muscular walls in the hands, and at last the whole belly is kneaded with the heel of the hand in a succession of rapid, deep movements, passing around in the direction of the colon.

It depends very much on the strength, endurance,

and practice of the manipulator how much good is done by these manœuvres. At first or for a few sittings they are to be very gentle, but by degrees they may be made more rough, and if the masseur be a good one it is astonishing how much strength may be used without hurting the patient.

The early treatments should last half an hour and should be increased by degrees to one hour, after which should follow an hour of absolute repose.

After the first few days I like the rubber to keep the part constantly lubricated with cocoa-oil, which is agreeable in odor, and which keeps well even in warm weather if a little lime-water be left standing on the top of it. Vaseline is also a good lubricant, and both of these agents make the skin smooth and soft and supple.

As soon as a part has been manipulated it should be at once wrapped up.

In men who are hairy it is often needful to have the limbs shaved, because the constant pull made on the hairs gives rise to very troublesome and painful boils.

The early use of massage is apt in some nervous women to cause increased nervousness and even loss of sleep; but these symptoms may safely be disregarded, because they pass away in a few days, and very soon the patient begins to find the massage delightfully soothing and to complain when it is omitted. Women who have a sensitive abdominal surface or ovarian tenderness have of course to be handled with care, but in a few days a practiced rubber will by degrees intrude upon the tender regions, and will end by kneading them with all desirable force. The same remarks apply to the spine when it is hurt by a touch, and it is very rare indeed to find persons whose irritable spots cannot at last be rubbed and kneaded to their permanent profit.

The daily massage is kept up through at least six weeks, and then, if everything seems to me to be going along well, I direct the rubber to spend half of the hour in exercising the limbs as a preparation for walking. This is done after the Swedish plan, by making movements of flexion and extension, which the patient is taught to resist.

At the seventh week the treatment is used on alternate days, and is commonly laid aside when the patient gets up and begins to move about.

During the past year, several of the members of the staff of the Infirmary for Nervous Disease, and especially my colleague, Dr. Wharton Sinkler, have obliged me by studying with care the influence of massage on temperature, and as to this some very interesting results have been obtained. In general, when we begin to rub a highly hysterical person the legs are apt to grow cold under the stimulation, and if this continues to be complained of it is no very good omen of the ultimate success of the treatment. But usually in a few days a change takes place, and the limbs all grow warm when kneaded, as happens in most people from the beginning of the treatment. The extreme low temperatures of the limbs of children suffering with so-called essential paralysis is well known. I have frequently seen these strangely cold parts rise, under an hour's massage, six to ten degrees F. In such small limbs, the long contact of a warm hand may account for at least a part of this notable rise in temperature.

In adults this can hardly be looked upon as a cause of the rise of temperature caused by massage, firstly, because the long exposure of large surfaces incident to the process is calculated to lessen whatever increase of heat the contact of the hand may cause, and secondly, because this rise is a very variable quantity, and because occasionally some other and less comprehensible factors actually induce a fall rather than a rise in the thermometer as a result of massage.

In very nervous or hysterical women, ignorant of

what the act of kneading may be expected to bring about, and especially in such as are thin and anæmic, and have either a somewhat high or an unusually low normal temperature, we may find at first a slight fall of the thermometer, then a fairly constant rise with some irregularities, and at last, as the health improves, a lessening effect or none at all.

The most notable rise is to be found in persons who, owing to some organic disease, have a natural liability to great changes of temperature.

I add a number of tables, which very well illustrate the facts just stated:

Mrs. J., at rest, on the usual diet. Manipulation at 11, daily.

Before Massage.	After Massage.
100	100
100	101⅕
99⅖	99⅘
99⅘	100
99⅖	100
100	100
99⅘	100
99⅘	100

Miss P., æt. 24, hysteria.

Before Massage.	After Massage.
99¼	99¼
98¼	99

Before Massage.	After Massage.
$98\frac{1}{2}$	99
$98\frac{1}{4}$	99
$98\frac{1}{4}$	$98\frac{1}{4}$
99	$99\frac{3}{4}$
$100\frac{1}{5}$	$100\frac{2}{5}$
$100\frac{2}{5}$	$101\frac{2}{5}$
$100\frac{2}{5}$	$100\frac{3}{5}$
$100\frac{3}{5}$	100

Mrs. L., a very thin, feeble, and bloodless woman, æt. 29 years.

Before Massage.	After Massage
99	100
$98\frac{1}{2}$	$99\frac{1}{5}$
98	$98\frac{2}{5}$
99	100
$98\frac{2}{5}$	$98\frac{4}{5}$
99	$99\frac{4}{5}$
100	$100\frac{1}{5}$
99	$99\frac{4}{5}$

Mrs. P., æt. 31, feeble and anæmic, nervous, slight albuminuria and chronic bronchitis. Liable to fever. 3 P.M.

Before Massage.	After Massage.
$101\frac{3}{5}$	102
100	$100\frac{4}{5}$
99	$99\frac{4}{5}$
100	101
$99\frac{2}{5}$	$100\frac{1}{5}$

Before Massage.	After Massage.
$99\frac{4}{5}$	$100\frac{3}{5}$
$100\frac{3}{5}$	$101\frac{3}{5}$
$100\frac{2}{5}$	$99\frac{4}{5}$
$100\frac{3}{5}$	$100\frac{2}{5}$
$100\frac{3}{10}$	$100\frac{9}{10}$
$99\frac{1}{5}$	$99\frac{4}{5}$

These temperatures were taken always before 4 P.M., and at intervals of three days. Her morning temperature was usually 99° to $99\frac{4}{5}$°, and in the evening, 9 to 10 o'clock, it always rose to 100, 101, and at times to 102.

As I have said already, there are persons who, under circumstances seemingly alike, have from massage a large rise of temperature, and others who experience none. I give a single case of what is rare but not exceptional, an almost constant fall of temperature.

Miss N., æt. 21, hysteria, good condition.

Before Massage.	After Massage.
98	$97\frac{3}{5}$
$98\frac{1}{2}$	$98\frac{1}{2}$
98	98
$98\frac{2}{5}$	98
$98\frac{4}{5}$	98

As menstruation is sometimes in very excitable people arrested by massage, I usually order the treatment to be given up during the flow. In the present case it was kept up without alteration of the rule as to fall of temperatures. These facts are, of course, extremely interesting, but it is well to add that the success of the treatment is not indicated in any constant way by the thermal changes, which are neither so steady nor so remarkable as those caused by electricity.

If now we ask ourselves why massage does good in cases of absolute rest, the answer—at least a partial answer—is not difficult. The secretions of the skin are stimulated by the treatment of that tissue, and it is visibly flushed, as it ought to be, from time to time by ordinary active exercise. Under massage the flabby muscles acquire a certain firmness, which at first lasts only for a few minutes, but which after a time is more enduring, and ends by becoming permanent. The firm grasp of the manipulator's hands stimulates the muscle, and, if sudden, causes it to contract sensibly. When the patient becomes used to the process, the operator is sometimes directed to strike the muscular masses with the soft cushion formed by the muscles on the ulnar side of the closed hand, or with the same part kept in rigid extension. The blow, if given adroitly, causes a momentary contraction of the muscle thus struck. The muscles are by these means exercised without the use of volition or the aid of the nervous centres, and at the same time the alternate grasp and relaxation of the manipulator's hands squeezes out the blood and allows it to flow back anew, thus healthfully exciting the vessels and increasing, mechanically, the flow of blood to the tissues which they feed.

The visible results as regards the surface circulation are sufficiently obvious, and most remarkably so in persons who, besides being anæmic and thin, have been long unused to exercise. After a few treatments the nails become pink, the veins show where before none were to be seen, the larger vessels grow fuller, and the whole tint of the limbs changes for the better.

In like manner the sore places, which either existed before or are brought into sensitive prominence by the manipulation, by degrees cease to be felt, and a general sensation of comfort and ease follows the later treatments.

I am accustomed to pay a good deal of attention to the observations made as to these and other points by practiced manipulators, and I find that their daily familiarity with every detail of the color and firmness of the tissues is often of great use to me.

CHAPTER VI.

ELECTRICITY.

ELECTRICITY is the second means which I have made use of for the purpose of exercising muscles in persons at rest. It has also an additional value, of which I shall presently speak.

In order to exercise the muscles best and with the least amount of pain and annoyance, we make use of an induction current, with interruptions as slow as one in every two to five seconds, a rate readily obtained in properly-constructed batteries. This plan is sure to give painless exercise, but it is less rapid and less complete as to the quality of the exercise caused than the movements evolved by very rapid interruptions. These, in the hands of a clever operator who knows his anatomy well, are therefore, on the whole, more satisfactory, but they require some experience to manage them so as not to shock and disgust the patient by inflicting needless pain. The poles, covered with well-wetted sponges, which I prefer to chamois or other thin covers, are placed on each muscle in turn, and kept about four inches apart. They are moved fast enough to allow of the muscles being well contracted, which is easily managed, and with sufficient speed if the assistant be thoroughly acquainted with the points of Ziemssen. After the legs are treated the muscles of the belly and back and loins are gone over systematically, and finally those of the chest and arms. The face and neck are neglected. About forty minutes to an hour are needed; but at first a less time is employed. The general result is to exercise in turn all the external muscles.

No such obvious and visible results are seen as we observe after massage, but the thermal changes are much more constant and remarkable, and show at least that we are not dealing with an agent which merely amuses the patient or acts alone through some mysterious influence on the mental status.

A half-hour's treatment of the muscles commonly gives rise to a marked elevation of temperature. which fades away within an hour or two. This effect is, like that from massage, most notable in persons liable to fever from some organic trouble, and it varies as to its degree in individuals who have no such disease.

The first case, Miss B., æt. 20, is an example of

tubercular disease of the apex of the right lung. She had a morning temperature of 98½ to 99½, and an evening temperature of 100 to 102.

Electricity was used about 11 o'clock daily, with these results:

	Before Electricity.	After Electricity.
November 25	99	99$\frac{3}{5}$
" 27	97$\frac{4}{5}$	100
" 28	98	99
" 29	98$\frac{3}{5}$	99$\frac{4}{5}$
December 2	100$\frac{1}{5}$	101$\frac{3}{5}$
" 4	99$\frac{1}{5}$	100$\frac{1}{5}$
" 5	99$\frac{2}{5}$	99$\frac{1}{5}$

Mrs. R., æt. 40, the next case, was merely a rather anæmic, feeble, and thin woman, who for years had not been able to endure any prolonged effort. She got well under the general treatment, gaining thirteen pounds on a weight of ninety-eight pounds, her height being five feet and one inch. The facts as to rise of temperature are most remarkable, and I need not say were carefully observed, the observations being made by Dr. Sinkler.

Temperature taken in the mouth while at rest in bed.

	Before Electricity.	After Electricity.
April 2	98$\frac{4}{5}$	98$\frac{4}{5}$
" 3	98$\frac{1}{5}$	98$\frac{2}{5}$
" 4	98$\frac{1}{5}$	98$\frac{2}{5}$

	Before Electricity	After Electricity	
April 5	98	$98\frac{4}{5}$	
" 6	$97\frac{9}{10}$	$98\frac{7}{10}$	
" 7	98	$98\frac{5}{10}$	
" 8	98	$98\frac{3}{5}$	
" 9	98	$99\frac{1}{10}$	
" 10	$98\frac{2}{5}$	$98\frac{3}{5}$	
" 11	$98\frac{5}{10}$	$98\frac{7}{10}$	
" 12	$98\frac{3}{5}$	$99\frac{1}{10}$	
" 13	$98\frac{1}{4}$	$99\frac{5}{10}$	
" 14	$98\frac{2}{5}$	$99\frac{1}{5}$	
" 16	$98\frac{4}{10}$	$99\frac{1}{10}$	
" 17	$98\frac{5}{10}$	$99\frac{2}{10}$	
" 18	$98\frac{7}{10}$	$99\frac{1}{10}$	one hour later, $99\frac{1}{10}$
" 19	$98\frac{9}{10}$	$99\frac{3}{10}$	" " " $98\frac{4}{5}$
" 20	99	$99\frac{1}{10}$	
" 21	$98\frac{9}{10}$	$99\frac{2}{10}$	
	Menstrual period.		
" 30	$98\frac{3}{4}$	$98\frac{3}{5}$	
May 1	98	$98\frac{5}{10}$	
" 2	98	$98\frac{3}{10}$	

The third case, Miss M., æt. 33, was that of a pallid woman, the daughter of a well-known physician in the south. She suffered for six years with "nervous exhaustion," headaches, pain in the back, intense depression of spirits, nausea, and repeated attacks of hysteria. She slept only under anodynes, and used stimulants freely. Under the use of rest and the adjuvant treatment described, Miss M. made a thorough recovery, and was restored to useful, active life.

Miss M. Thermometer held in mouth five minutes before and after treatment.

	Before Electricity.	After Electricity.	
May 14	$99\frac{1}{10}$	$99\frac{1}{10}$	} Menstruating; general faradi-
" 15	99	$99\frac{1}{5}$	} zation only.
" 16	$99\frac{1}{5}$	$99\frac{1}{5}$	Gen'l faradization and limbs.
" 17	$98\frac{4}{5}$	$99\frac{1}{5}$	
" 18	$98\frac{4}{5}$	$99\frac{1}{5}$	
" 19	$98\frac{1}{5}$	$98\frac{4}{5}$	
" 21	$98\frac{3}{5}$	99	
" 22	$98\frac{4}{5}$	$99\frac{1}{10}$	
" 25	$98\frac{1}{10}$	$98\frac{4}{10}$	
" 26	$98\frac{1}{10}$	$99\frac{1}{10}$	
" 29	$98\frac{3}{5}$	99	
" 30	$98\frac{5}{10}$	$99\frac{1}{10}$	
" 31	$98\frac{9}{10}$	$99\frac{1}{10}$	

Mrs. P., æt. 38, was a rather nervous woman, easily tired, but not anæmic and not very thin. She improved greatly under the treatment.

Mrs. P. General tonic treatment.

	Before Electricity.	After Electricity.	
January 27	$98\frac{3}{5}$	$99\frac{1}{5}$	Thermometer in axilla ten
" 29	$98\frac{2}{5}$	$99\frac{1}{5}$	minutes before and after.
" 30	$99\frac{1}{5}$	$99\frac{3}{5}$	
" 31	$98\frac{4}{5}$	$99\frac{2}{5}$	
February 1	99	$99\frac{2}{5}$	

Menstrual period.

	Before Electricity.	After Electricity.	
February 8	$98\frac{2}{5}$	$99\frac{1}{5}$	
" 9	$98\frac{3}{5}$	99	
" 10	$98\frac{3}{5}$	99	
" 12	$98\frac{1}{5}$	$99\frac{2}{5}$	
" 13	$98\frac{2}{5}$	99	
" 14	$98\frac{2}{5}$	$98\frac{3}{5}$	
" 15	$98\frac{2}{5}$	$98\frac{4}{5}$	
" 19	99	$98\frac{2}{5}$	
" 20	98	99	
" 23	$98\frac{3}{5}$	$99\frac{1}{5}$	Thermometer in mouth five
" 24	99	$99\frac{3}{5}$	minutes before and after.
" 27	$99\frac{1}{5}$	$99\frac{3}{5}$	
" 28	$98\frac{4}{5}$	$99\frac{2}{5}$	

Menstrual period.

	Before Electricity.	After Electricity.
March 13	99	$99\frac{1}{5}$
" 14	$98\frac{4}{5}$	$98\frac{4}{5}$
" 15	99	$99\frac{1}{5}$

Miss R., æt. 27, was a fair case of hysterical conditions; overuse of chloral and bromides; anorexia and loss of flesh and color.

Thermometer held in mouth five minutes before and after treatment.

	Before Electricity.	After Electricity.	
May 15	100	100	General faradization for fifteen minutes.
" 16	100	100	
" 17	$100\frac{1}{5}$	$100\frac{2}{5}$	
" 18	$98\frac{2}{5}$	$98\frac{3}{5}$	Gen'l faradization and arm muscles twenty minutes.
" 19	$99\frac{4}{5}$	$100\frac{1}{10}$	

70 ELECTRICITY.

	Before Electricity.	After Electricity.	
May 20	$100\frac{1}{10}$	100	General faradization, ten
" 22	$99\frac{2}{5}$	$99\frac{1}{5}$	minutes; arms and legs,
" 26	$99\frac{1}{10}$	$99\frac{6}{10}$	twenty minutes.
" 27	$99\frac{3}{10}$	$99\frac{4}{10}$	
" 28	$99\frac{2}{5}$	$99\frac{2}{5}$	
" 29	$99\frac{3}{10}$	$99\frac{3}{10}$	
" 30	$99\frac{1}{10}$	$99\frac{4}{10}$	
" 31	$99\frac{1}{10}$	$99\frac{2}{10}$	
June 2	$99\frac{2}{5}$	$99\frac{1}{5}$	
" 4	$99\frac{5}{10}$	$99\frac{6}{10}$	
" 6	$99\frac{3}{10}$	$99\frac{5}{10}$	
" 7	$99\frac{3}{10}$	$99\frac{5}{10}$	

I have given these full details because I have not seen elsewhere any statement of the rather remarkable phenomena which they exemplify. It may be that a part at least of the thermal change is due to the muscular action, although this seems hardly competent to account for any large share in the alteration of temperature, and we must look further to explain it fully. No mental excitement can be called upon as a cause, since it continues after the patient is perfectly accustomed to the process. I should add, also, that in most cases the subject of the experiment was kept in ignorance of the fact that a rise of the thermometer was to be expected. Is it not possible that the current even of an induction battery has the power so to stimulate the tissues as to cause an increase in the ordinary rate of disintegrative change? Perhaps a careful study of the secretions might lend force to this suggestion. That the muscular action produced by the battery is not essential to cause increase of the bodily heat is shown by the next set of facts to which I desire to call attention.

Some years ago Messrs. Beard and Rockwell stated that when an induced current is used for fifteen to thirty minutes daily, one pole on the neck and one on either foot, or alternately on both, the persistent use of this form of treatment was decidedly tonic in its influence. I believe that in this opinion they were perfectly correct, and I am now able to show at least that, thus employed, the induced current causes also a decided rise of temperature in many people, which proves at least that it is in some way an active agent, capable of positively influencing the nutritive changes of the body.

The rise of temperature thus caused is less constant, as well as less marked, than that caused by the muscle treatment. I do not think it necessary to give the tables in full. They show in the best cases rises of one-fifth to four-fifths of a degree F., and were taken with the very utmost care, to exclude all possible causes of error.

The mode of treatment is as follows: At the close

of the muscle electrization one pole is placed on the nape of the neck and one on a foot for fifteen minutes. Then the foot pole is shifted to the other foot and left for a length of time.

The primary current is used as being less painful, and the interruptions are made as rapid as possible, while the control wires or cylinder are adjusted so as to give a current which is not uncomfortable.

I have been asked very often if all of the means here described be necessary, and I have been criticised by some of the reviewers of my first edition because I had not pointed out the relative needfulness of the various agencies employed. In fact, I have made very numerous clinical studies of cases, in some of which I used rest, seclusion, and massage, and in others rest, seclusion, and electricity. It is, of course, difficult, I may say impossible, to state in any numerical manner the reason for my conclusion in favor of the conjoined use of all of these means. If one is to be left out, I have no hesitation in saying that it should be electricity.

CHAPTER VII.

DIETETICS AND THERAPEUTICS.

The somewhat wearisome and minute details I have given as to Seclusion, Rest, Massage, and Electricity, have prepared the way for a discussion of the dietetic and medicinal treatment which without them would be neither possible nor useful.

As to diet, we have to be guided by the previous condition and history of the patient.

Very rarely these women are good feeders, and those who are, seem apt to be—in a few cases—fat as well as anæmic. As to this latter class, it is needful to say something before we consider the larger group. I have sought to treat fat anæmic cases by the use of massage, electricity, iron, and rest, but this does not answer so well as another plan, which at first sight may seem somewhat startling. After putting the patients at absolute rest in bed I place them on a diet of skimmed milk, which is kept at such an amount as will thin the woman at a rate that will cost her about half a pound daily.

If she were afoot this falling off would be severely felt, but when abed it is amazing how little annoyance it causes.

As to the detail of treatment, it is as follows: The rest is made absolute, as to which I have already spoken. Then I give daily about two quarts of milk, well skimmed. It is used as Carel directs, cold or warm, not hot, and the amount given is divided so that the patient takes every two hours enough to make up the full share during the waking day. In my hospital wards we weigh the patient every day, and the milk is slowly reduced until the loss of weight becomes perceptible. When a woman weighing one hundred pounds is lying in bed, and does nothing, about three pints of skimmed milk daily will usually sustain her weight without other nourishment; but as to this, there are, of course, individual peculiarities. M. C., æt. 22, a very nervous person, with some dyspepsia, was thus fed, and for ten days did not vary more than a few ounces from day to day.

I saw lately a lady from New York, who, having been dyspeptic, was placed on milk diet, and for two years lived a moderately active life afoot on two quarts of milk per diem. She consulted me as to the method of escaping from the tiresome monotony of this diet. As I observed that while exercising she was unable to digest other food without pain, I put her at rest and used massage and electricity. After a time I treated her as I would have done a child who had to be rapidly weaned, and was thus successful by a series of changes in diet in enabling her to increase to a sufficient and comfortable extent the range of her dietary.

When using milk as a restricted diet in cases of fatness with anæmia, it is sometimes necessary to substitute beef-soup for a day at a time on account of the disgust which milk may occasion.

Early this spring, Mrs. C., æt. 40, came under my care with partial hysterical paralysis of the right and hemi-anæsthesia of the left side. She had no power to feel pain or to distinguish heat from cold, but touch was perfect. The long strain of great moral suffering had left her in this state, and rendered her somewhat emotional. Her appetite was fair, but she was strangely white, and weighed one hundred and sixty-three pounds, with a height of five feet five inches. As she had had endless treatment by iron, change of air, and the like, I did not care to repeat what had already failed. She was therefore put at rest in bed, and treated with milk, slowly lessened in amount. Her stomach-troubles, which had been very annoying, at once disappeared, and when the milk fell to three pints she began to lose flesh. With a quart of milk a day she lost half a pound daily, and in two weeks her weight fell to one hundred and forty pounds. She was then placed on the full treatment, which I shall hereafter describe. The weight returned slowly, and with it she became quite ruddy, while her flesh lost altogether its flabby character. I never saw a more striking or more instructive result.

I have been careful to speak at length of these fat anæmic cases because, while rare, they have been, to me, at least, among the most difficult to manage of all the curable anæmias, and because with the plan described I have been almost as successful as I could desire.

The use of milk makes nearly always an essential part of my early treatment of the mass of my cases. I mean of those who are thin and anæmic.

Let us suppose that we have carefully studied a case and decided that we have to deal with a person who is thin-blooded, feeble, and lacks flesh. Let us make sure that there is no grave uterine or other malady, no renal or pulmonary disease, nothing worse than constant dyspepsia and the numberless aches and tires which characterize these patients. We separate the woman from her friends, and we put her at entire rest in bed.

The next step is to get her by degrees on a milk diet, which has two advantages. It enables us to know precisely the amount of food taken, and to regulate it easily; and it nearly always dismisses, as by magic, all the dyspeptic conditions. If the case be an old one I rarely omit the milk; but, although I begin with three ounces every two hours, I increase it in a few days up to two quarts, given in divided doses every three hours. If a cup of coffee given without sugar on awaking does not regulate the bowels, I add a small amount of watery extract of aloes at bedtime; or if the constipation be obstinate, I give thrice a day one quarter of a grain of ex. aloës with two grains of dried ox-gall. I find the simple milk diet a great aid towards getting rid of chloral, bromides, and morphia, all of which I usually am able to lay aside during the first week of treatment. Nor is it less easy with the same means to enable the patient to give up stimulus, and I may add that in the congested stomach of the habitual hard drinker the milk treatment is of admirable efficacy. As I have spoken over and over of the use of stimulus by nervous women, I should be careful to explain that anything like great excess on the part of women of the upper classes is, in my opinion, extremely rare, and that when I speak of the habit of stimulation I mean only that nervous women are apt to be taught to take wine or whisky daily, to an extent that does not affect visibly their appearance or demeanor.

Meanwhile the mechanical treatment is steadily pursued, and in four days to a week, when the stomach has become comfortable, I order the patient to take also a light breakfast. In a day or two she is given a mutton-chop as a midday dinner, and in a day or two more she has added bread and butter thrice a day; within ten days I am commonly able to allow three full meals daily, as well as three or four pints of milk, which are given at and after meals, in place of water.

Within ten days I order also two ounces of fluid malt extract before each meal. I have tried all the extracts, but I prefer the imported Hoff's fluid malt.

No troublesome symptoms usually result from this full feeding, and the patient is made to eat more largely by being fed by her attendant. People who will eat very little if they feed themselves, often take a large amount when fed by another, and, as I have said before, nothing is more tiresome than for a patient flat on her back to cut up her food, and to use the fork or spoon. By the plan of feeding we thus gain doubly.

As to the meals, I leave them to the patient's caprice, unless this is too unreasonable; but I like to give butter largely, and as it is with us very good, I have little trouble in getting this most wholesome fat taken in large amounts.

At the close of the first week I like to add one pound of beef, in the form of raw soup. This is made by chopping up one pound of raw beef, placing it in a bottle with one pint of water and five drops of strong chlorohydric acid. This mixture stands on ice all night, and in the morning the bottle is set in a pan of water at 110° F., and kept two hours at about this temperature. It is then thrown on to a stout cloth and strained until the mass which remains is nearly dry. The filtrate is given in three portions daily. If the raw taste prove very objectionable, the beef to be used is quickly roasted on one side, and then the process is completed in the manner above described. The soup thus made is for the most part raw, but has also the flavor of cooked meat.

In difficult cases, especially those treated in cool weather, I sometimes add, at the third week, one half-ounce of cod-liver oil, given half an hour after each meal. If it lessens the appetite, or causes nausea, I use it thrice a day as a rectal injection; and in cases where the large doses of iron used cause intense constipation, I find the use of cod-oil enemata doubly valuable, by acting as a nutriment and by disposing the bowels to act daily. When given thus, I like to use it in emulsion, with the juice drained off after crushing the fresh pancreas of the beef in warm water. Enough water to cover a half-pound of chopped pancreas is allowed to stand for an hour in a warm kitchen, and then squeezed through a towel. An ounce is mixed with half that amount of oil and injected slowly thrice a day. This suits some people well, and may result in a single passage daily, but in others it is annoying, and is either badly retained or not at all, and sometimes gives rise to tenesmus.

The question of stimulus is a grave one. In too many cases which come to me, I have to give so much care to break off the use of all forms of alcoholic drinks that I am loath to resort to them in any case, although I am satisfied that a small amount is a help towards speedy increase of fat. It is, therefore, a matter for careful judgment, and in persons who have never used it in excess, or as a habit, I prefer to give, with the other treatment, a small daily ration of stimulus; an ounce a day of whisky, or two or three glasses of dry champagne have seemed to me useful as adjuvants, and as increasing the capacity to take food at meals. Nevertheless, alcohol is not essential in these cases, and, for the most part, I give none, except the small amount found in malt extracts.

So soon as my patient begins to take other food than milk, and sometimes even before this, I like to give iron; but I have not much faith in the grain doses of iron in common use, and, after many trials, I find that the old subcarbonate of iron of the United States Pharmacopœia answers every purpose, and has the advantages, for hospital use, of cheapness, and of being not unpalatable.

I order two ounces of the powder to be put in one quart of distilled water. This is well shaken, and two ounces poured into a half-tumbler of water, or carbonated water, or apollinaris water. This is drunk at each meal, and, in some cases, four or five times a day.

Very often I meet with women who cannot take iron, either because it disturbs the stomach, causes headache, or constipates, or else because Dr. Blank has told them never to take iron. In the latter case I simply add five grains of pyrophosphate to each ounce of malt, and give it thus for a month unknown to the patient. It is then easy to make clear to them that iron is not so difficult to take as they had been led to believe, and when it has ceased to disagree mentally, I find that I am able to fall back on the coarser method. If iron constipates, as it may and does often do when used in these large doses, the trouble is corrected by the pill of aq. ex. aloës and gall already mentioned, or by the enemata of oil. The instances in which iron gives headache and sense of fulness are very rare when the patient is undergoing the full treatment described, and, as a rule, I disregard all such complaints, and find that after a time I cease to hear anything more of the symptoms alluded to. Of late I have also used with increasing satisfaction dialyzed oxide of iron.[1] It does not color the teeth, and I do not think it constipates as much as the subcarbonate, and many of my patients think it suits them better than any other form of iron. I give it four times a day, in doses of six to nine grains.

Unless some especial need arises, iron, in some form, is the only drug I care to use in these cases until the patient begins to sit up, when I give nearly

---

[1] This is now admirably made, on a large scale, by Wyeth & Co., of Philadelphia.

DIETETICS AND THERAPEUTICS. 83

always the thirtieth of a grain of strych. sulph. thrice a day.

Probably no physician will read the account I have here detailed of the vast amount of food which I am enabled to give, not only with impunity from dyspepsia, but with lasting advantage, without some sense of wonder; and, for my own part, I can only say that I have watched again and again, with growing surprise, some listless, feeble, white-blooded creature learning by degrees to consume these large rations, and gathering under their use flesh, color, and wholesomeness of mind and body. It is needless to say that it is not in all cases easy to carry out this treatment.

When the full treatment has been reached, and kept up for a few days, I begin to watch the urine with care, because, if the patient be over-fed, the renal secretion speedily betrays this result in the precipitation of urates. When this occurs at all steadily, I usually give directions to lessen the amount of nitrogenous food until the urine is again free from sediment.

Nearly always at some time in the progress of the case there are attacks of dyspepsia, when it suffices to cut down the diet one-half, or to give milk alone for a day or two. Diarrhœa is more rare, and has to be met in like manner; or, if obstinate, it may be requisite to give the milk boiled. Occasionally the rapid increase of blood is shown by nasal hemorrhage, which needs no especial treatment.

Perhaps I shall make myself more clear if I now relate in full the diet-list of some of my cases, and the mode of arranging it.

I take the following case as an illustration from my note-book:

Mrs. C., a New England woman, undertook, at the age of sixteen, a severe course of study, and in two years completed the whole range of studies, which, at the school she went to, were usually spread over four years. An early marriage; three pregnancies, the last two of which broke in upon the year of nursing; began at last to show in loss of flesh and color. Meanwhile she met with energy the multiplied claims of a life full of sympathy for every form of trouble, and, neglecting none of the duties of society or kinship, she yet found time for study and accomplishments. By and by she began to feel tired, and at last gave way quite abruptly, ceased to menstruate five years before I saw her, grew pale and feeble, and dropped in weight in six months from one hundred and twenty-five pounds to ninety-five. Nature had at last its revenge. Everything wearied her: to eat, to drive, to read, to sew. Walking became impossible, and, tied to her couch, she grew dyspeptic and constipated. The asthenopia which is almost constantly seen in such cases added to her trials, because reading had to be abandoned, and so at last, despite unusual vigor of character, she gave way to utter despair, and became at times emotional and morbid in her views of life. After numberless forms of treatment had been used in vain, she came to this city and passed into my care.

At this time she could not walk more than a few steps without flushing and without a sense of painful tire. Her temperature was 97°.5 F., and her white corpuscles were perhaps a third too numerous. After most careful examination I could find no disease of any one organ, and I therefore advised a resort to the treatment with full confidence in the result.

In this single case I give the schedule of diet in full as a fair example:

October 10.—Mrs. C. remained in bed at entire rest. She was fed, and rose only for the purpose of relieving the bladder or the rectum.

10.—Took one quart of milk in divided doses every two hours.

11.—A cup of coffee on rising, and two quarts of milk given in divided portions every two hours. A pill of aloes every night, which answered for a few days.

12 to 15.—Same diet. The dyspepsia by this time was relieved, and she slept without her habitual dose of chloral. The pint of raw soup was added in three proportions on the 16th.

17 and 18.—Same diet.

19.—She took, on awaking at 7, coffee; at 7.30, half-pint of milk; and the same at 10 A.M., 12 M., 2, 4, 6, 8, and 10 P.M. The soup at 11, 5, and 9.

23.—She took for breakfast an egg and bread and butter; and two days later (25th) dinner was added, and the iron.

On the 28th this was the schedule:

On waking, coffee at 7. At 8, iron and malt. Breakfast, a chop, bread and butter; of milk, a tumbler and a half. At 11, soup. At 2, iron and malt. Dinner, closing with milk, one or two tumblers. The dinner consisted of anything she liked, and with it she took about six ounces of burgundy or dry champagne. At 4, soup. At 7, malt, iron, bread and butter, and usually some fruit, and commonly two glasses of milk. At 9, soup; and at 10 her aloe pill. At 12 M., massage occupied an hour. At 4.30 P.M. electricity was used for an hour in the manner which I have described.

This heavy diet-list, reached in a few days by a woman who had been unable to digest with comfort the lightest meal, seemed certainly surprising. I have not given in full the amount eaten at meal-time. Small at first, it was increased rapidly by the patient's growing desire for food, and became in a few days three full meals.

It is necessary to see the result in one of these successful cases in order to credit it. Mrs. C. began to show gain in flesh about the face in the second week of treatment, and during her two months in bed rose in weight from ninety-six pounds to one hundred and thirty-six; nor was the gain in color less marked.

At the sixth week of treatment the soup was dropped, wine abandoned, the iron lessened one-half, the massage and electricity used on alternate days, and the limbs exercised as I have described. The usual precautions as to rising and exercise were carefully attended to, and at the ninth week of treatment my patient took a drive. At this time all mechanical treatment ceased, the milk was reduced to a quart, the iron to five grains thrice a day, and the malt continued. At the sixth week I began to employ strychnia in doses of one-thirtieth of a grain thrice a day at meals, and this was kept up for several months, together with the iron and malt. The cure was complete and permanent, and its character may be tested by the fact that at the thirtieth day of rest in bed, and after five years of failure to menstruate, to her surprise she menstruated, and continued to do so with regularity until eighteen months later, when she became pregnant. The only drawback to her perfect use of all her functions lay in asthenopia, which persisted nearly a year after she left my care. Fatigue of vision for near work is a common condition of the cases I am now describing, and it is apt to persist long after all other troubles have vanished. When there is no asthenopia I usually think well of the general chance of recovery; but in no case of feeble vision do I omit to have the optical apparatus of the eye looked at with care, because pure asthenopia, apart from all optical defects, is a somewhat rare symptom.

In thus stating the schedule of diet and treatment I do not wish it to be considered as applicable to all cases. There are rare, very rare, cases in which milk agrees best between meals. There are cases, still more rare, in which no milk can be taken under any circumstances. There are others in which cod-liver oil is known to agree so well that it can be given in unusual doses.

As additional illustrations I shall now state a few cases, and I shall not enter into minute details of treatment.

The following case is reported by Dr. John Keating, who watched it with care throughout:

Mr. P. D., æt. 53, after more than thirty years of close attention to business, which severely tried both mental and physical endurance, found himself, in January, 1877, at the close of some months of gradually increasing feebleness, absolutely unable to fulfil his usual duties, and the most alarming symptoms manifested themselves. There was utter prostration of nervous and muscular force; his limbs refused their support; his appetite failed; the recollection of ordinary phrases involved distinct and painful effort; sleep became unattainable, except under the influence of powerful narcotics, and even that brief slumber was rendered valueless by the incessant convulsive twitching of the muscles.

His physician prescribed iron and strychnia; ordered an immediate abandonment of all business and instant departure to a point where telegraph wires were unknown and mails infrequent. He went at once to the Bahamas, passing a month in that delicious climate in absolute inaction; more than another month was consumed in slowly returning, but, though some flesh had been gained, there was only a trifling improvement in the nervous condition.

May 1, 1877, Dr. Mitchell examined Mr. P. D. The patient was sallow and emaciated, and coughed every few moments. He had night-sweats, nervous twitching, and slight dulness on percussion at the apex of the right lung, with prolonged expiration and roughened inspiration, and some increase of vocal resonance.

Mr. P. D. was allowed to be out of bed once a day four hours, and to spend one at his place of business. The treatment was as follows:

At 6 A.M., a tumbler of strong, hot beef-tea, made from the Australian extract.

At 8 A.M., half a tumbler of iron-water, and breakfast, consisting of fruit, steak, potatoes, coffee, and a goblet of milk.

At 8.30 A.M., a goblet of milk mixed with a dessert-spoonful of Loefland's extract of malt, with 6 grains of citrate of iron and quinine.

At 10 o'clock Dr. Keating administered the electricity.

At 12 o'clock Mr. P. D. might be dressed, making as little personal effort as possible. The second goblet of milk and malt was administered, and a carriage took him to his office, where he might remain till 2 o'clock, when the carriage brought him for dinner, preceded by half a tumbler of iron-water. All walking was forbidden.

After dinner (which included a goblet of milk) the third goblet of milk and malt was swallowed; then a short drive might be taken, but by 4 o'clock the patient must be undressed and in bed.

At 6 P.M. the third dose of iron-water presented itself, and a light supper of fruit, bread and butter, and cream, followed by the fourth goblet of milk and malt. Two quarts of milk were thus swallowed every day in addition to all other food.

At 9 P.M., massage one hour, with cocoa oil, followed by beef-soup, four ounces.

At the fourth week the soup was given up; dialyzed iron substituted for all other forms. June 4, electricity was given up. The malt was continued until June 20.

May 6, Mr. D. weighed in heavy winter dress one hundred and twenty-five pounds; June 20, in the lightest summer garb, he weighed one hundred and thirty-three pounds; in August it rose to one hundred and forty pounds, and he has continued to gain. He is strong and well, has no cough, and has ceased to be what he had been for years—a delicate man.

I am in debt to Professor Goodell for the following case, which I never saw, but which was carried on with every detail of my treatment. As the testimony of an admirable observer, it is valuable evidence. Professor Goodell writes as follows:

"Dear Doctor Mitchell:

"You asked me to give you the history of one of my patients who was cured by the treatment you so warmly advocate. I gladly do so, because it is a typical example of what your treatment can effect.

"Some four years ago, Mrs. Y., a very highly intelligent lady, from a neighboring city, came to consult me. She suffered dreadfully at each monthly period, and had constant ovarian pains and a wearying back-ache, which kept her on a lounge most of the day. She was also barren, and altogether in a pitiable condition. After a two months' treatment she returned home very much better, and soon after conceived. As pregnancy advanced many of her old symptoms came back, but it was hoped that maternity would rid her of them. The shock of the labor, however, proved too great for her already shattered nervous system. She became far more wretched than before, and again sought my advice.

"At this time I found all her old pains and aches running riot. She got no relief from them night or day without large doses of chloral. The slightest exertion, such as sewing, writing, and reading for a few minutes, greatly wearied her. Even the simple mental effort of casting up the weekly housekeeping expenses of a very small household upset her, and she had to give it up. The act of walking one of our squares, or of going down a short flight of stairs, or of riding for an hour in a well-padded carriage, gave her such 'unspeakable agony'—to use her own words—that she would have a hysterical attack of screams and tears. So emotional had this constant nerve-strain made her that she could not sustain an ordinary conversation without giving way to tears. Much of her time was spent in bed; in fact, she was practically bedridden.

"I tried in vain to wean her from her anodynes, and failed altogether in doing her any good, although many remedies were resorted to, and various modes of treatment adopted. Finally, in sheer despair, I put her to bed, and began your treatment of rest, with electricity, massage, and frequent feeding. The first trace of improvement showed itself in a greater self-control, and in a lessening of her aches and pains. Next, smaller doses of the anodyne were needed, until it was wholly withheld. Then she began to pick up an appetite, which, towards the close of the treatment, became so keen that, between three good meals every day, she drank several goblets of milk and of beef-tea. At the outset I had stipulated for six weeks of this treatment, and it was with reluctance that my patient yielded to my wish. But when the time was up she had become so impressed with the wonderful benefits she had received and was receiving, that she begged to have the treatment continued for two weeks more. At the end of that time she had gained at least thirty pounds in weight, and had lost every pain and ache. Her night-terrors, which I forgot to mention as one of her distressing symptoms, had wholly disappeared, and she could sleep from nine to ten hours at a stretch. I now sent her into the country, where she is continuing to mend, and is astonishing her friends by her scrambles up and down the steep hills.

"Such were the salient features of this case, and I can assure you that I was as much impressed by the happy results of the treatment as were a host of anxious and doubting friends.

"Very faithfully yours,
"WM. GOODELL."

Miss C., an interesting woman, æt. 26, at the age of 20 passed through a grave trial in the shape of nursing her mother through a typhoid fever. Soon after, a series of calamities deprived her of fortune, and she became, for support, a clerk, and did for two years eight hours of work daily. Under these successive strains her naturally sturdy health gave way. First came the pain in the back, then growing paleness, loss of flesh, and unending sense of tire. Her work, which was a necessity, was of course kept up, steadily at first, but was soon interrupted by increase of the menstrual flow, with unusual pain and persistent ovarian tenderness. Very soon she began to drop her work for a day at a time. Then came an increasing asthenopia with evening headaches, until her temper changed and became capricious and irritable. When I saw her she had been forced to abandon all labor and had been treated by an accomplished gynæcologist, and was said to be cured of a prolapsus uteri and of extensive ulceration, despite which relief she gained nothing in vigor and endurance, and got back neither color nor flesh.

She went to bed December 10 and rose for the first time February 4, having gained twenty-nine pounds. She went to bed pale and got up actually ruddy. In a month she returned to her work again, and has remained ever since in health which enables her, as she writes me, "to enjoy work, and to do with myself what I like."

Two years ago Miss L., æt. 26, came to me with the following history: At the age of 20 she had a fall, and began in a week or two to have an irritable spine. Then, after a few months, a physician advised rest, to which she took only too kindly, and in a year from the time of her accident she was rarely out of bed. Surrounded by highly sympathetic relatives, to whom chronic illness was somewhat novel, she speedily developed with their tender aid hyperæsthetic states of the eye and ear, so that her nurses crept about in a darkened room, the piano was silenced, and the children kept quiet. By slow degrees a whole household passed under the selfish despotism of a hysterical girl. Intense constipation, anorexia, and alternate states of dysuria, aneuria, and polyuria followed, and before long her sister began to fail in health, owing to the incessant exactions to which she too willingly yielded. This alarmed a brother, who insisted upon a change of treatment, and after some months she was brought on a couch to this city.

At the time I first saw her she took thirty grains of chloral every night and three hypodermic injections of one-half grain of morphia daily. As to food, she took next to none, and I could only guess her weight at about ninety pounds. She was in height five feet two and a half inches, and very sallow, with pale lips, and the large, indented tongue of anæmia. I made the most careful search for signs of organic mischief, and finding none, I began my treatment as usual with milk, and added massage and electricity without waiting. Her digestion seemed so good that I gave the iron in twenty-grain doses from the third day, and also the aloe extract pill thrice a day. It is perhaps needless to state that I isolated her with a nurse she had never seen before, and that for seven weeks she saw no one else save myself and the attendants. The full schedule of diet was reached at the end of a fortnight, and the chloral and morphia were given up at the second day. She slept well the fourth night, and, save twice a slight return of polyuria, she went on without a single drawback. In two months she was afoot and weighed one hundred and twenty-one pounds. Her change in tint, flesh, and expression was so remarkable that the process of repair might well have been called a renewal of life.

She went home changed no less morally than physically, and resumed her place in the family circle and in social life, a healthy and well-cured woman.

I might multiply these histories almost endlessly. In some cases I have cured without fattening; in others, though rarely, the mental habits formed through years of illness have been too deeply ingrained for change, and I have seen the patient get up fat and well only to relapse on some slight occasion.

The intense persistency with which some women study and dwell upon their symptoms is often the great difficulty. Even a slight physical annoyance becomes for one of these unhappily constituted natures a grave and almost ineradicable trouble, owing to the habit of self-study.

Miss P., æt. 29, weight one hundred and eleven pounds, height five feet four inches, dark-skinned, sallow, and covered with the acne of bromidism, consulted me last year. She had had one attack which some one considered to have been epileptic, and which was probably hysterical, but on this matter she dwelt with incessant terror, which was fostered by the tender care of a near relative, who left her neither by night nor day. Vague neuralgic aches in the limbs, with constant weariness, asthenopia, anæmia, loss of appetite, and loss of flesh, followed. Then came spinal pain and irregular menstruation, a long course of local cauterizations of the womb, spinal braces, and endless tonics and narcotics.

I broke up the association which had nearly been fatal to both women, and, confidently promising a cure, carried out my treatment in full. In three months she went home well and happy, greatly improved in looks, her skin clear, her functions regular, and weighing one hundred and thirty-six pounds.

It is vain to repeat the relation of such cases, and impossible to put on paper the means for deciding—what is so large a part of success in treatment—the moral methods of obtaining confidence and insuring a childlike acquiescence in every needed measure.

Another class of cases will, however, bear some further illustration. We meet with women who are healthy in mind, but who have some chronic pain or some definite malady which does not get well, either because the usual tonics fail, or because their occupations in life keep them always in a state of exhaustion. If, by rest, we slow the machinery, and by massage and electricity deprive rest of its evils, we can often obtain cures which are to be had in no other way. This is true of many uterine and some other disorders.

Miss B., æt. 37, height five feet five inches, weight one hundred and fifteen pounds, a school-teacher, without any notable organic disease, had a severe fall, owing to an accident while driving. A slight swelling in the hurt lumbar region was followed by pain, which became intense when she walked any distance. Loss of color, flesh, and appetite ensued, and after much treatment she consulted me, a year and a half ago. I could find nothing beyond soreness on deep pressure, and she was anything but hysterical or emotional.

Two months' rest with the usual treatment brought her weight up to one hundred and thirty-eight pounds, and she has been able ever since to do her usual work, and to walk when and where and as far as she wished.

A year ago I treated with some reluctance a lady who had extensive bronchitis and a slight albuminuria. This woman was a mere skeleton, with every function out of order. I undertook her case with the utmost distrust, but I had the pleasure to find her fattening and reddening like others. Her cough left her, the albumen disappeared, and she became well enough to walk and drive; when a sudden congestion of the kidneys destroyed her in forty-eight hours.

I have ventured, without much hope, to treat three cases of phthisis in the same manner. There are cases of this nature in which exercise wearies.

There are others which we cannot for various reasons send away to more genial climates, and in such instances we are driven to merely watch the slow decline of our patients. I believe that sometimes, and especially in the very earliest stages of consumption, my treatment will save a small percentage of such people, but, as yet, I only venture to make the suggestion, and wish distinctly to state that my experience in this form of its usefulness is limited.

One of the cases treated got well and remained well. There was every evidence of pulmonary trouble.

No. 2 improved enormously in all respects, and relapsed hopelessly, owing to large and repeated bleeding from piles and rectal fissure.

No. 3, a male, at 24 was treated by rest and massage without electricity, and improved so as to resume his work. He still has slight cough, and has to be careful, and there are, as yet, distinct evidences of inactive disease at the summit of the left lung.

To save further details, I give a brief summary of eight cases of women, all of whom were thin, feeble, anæmic, and vexed with some of the endless variety of pains, aches, and ailments, real, imaginary, or exaggerated by attention, which so constantly mark these cases.

Mrs. L., æt. 29, in three months gained eighteen pounds, and became well and vigorous.

Miss R., æt. 28, in two months gained twenty-one pounds, and from a bed-ridden invalid became a strong and quite ruddy woman.

Miss L., æt. 29, height five feet eight inches, weight one hundred and eighteen pounds, in four months became perfectly well, and rose in weight to one hundred and sixty-nine pounds. Two months were spent in bed.

Miss E., a nervous, morbid invalid, with a threat of insanity and a wretched state of mind and body, became quite florid, and rose in weight to one hundred and thirty-two pounds from one hundred and nineteen pounds.

Mrs. P., a case of curious and incessant sense of fatigue on walking or standing, gained in six weeks sixteen pounds, but was merely improved, and not cured.

Miss M., æt. 32, at one time a bright, cheerful woman, had a slight fall, and some moral strains, which speedily reduced her to a state of invalidism, and made her so irritable and morbid that she became a source of misery alike to herself and others. She was well cured in nine weeks of rest, and became of a good color, but did not gain over seven pounds.

Miss B., a school-teacher, treated at the Infirmary, was not anæmic. She had, however, the usual train of nervous symptoms, with irritable spine. She gained thirteen pounds in seven weeks, and seems well, but as yet has not tested her endurance by a return to work.

Mrs. R., æt. 38, height five feet three inches, weight one hundred and ten pounds, was never bedridden, but was obliged to lie down several hours a day. She was highly nervous, dreadfully dyspeptic, and singularly anæmic. She was made able to do what she pleased, except that I am obliged to insist on four hours of daily rest. Her change in color was remarkable, and she gained twenty-five pounds in nine weeks.

I could give other cases of gain in flesh without manifest relief. As I have said, these are rare, but it is less uncommon to see great relief without improvement in weight at all, or until the patient is up and afoot for some weeks.

I have mentioned, more than once, the singular return of menstruation under this treatment, and as examples I add a brief list of the most notable instances.

Mrs. N., æt. 29, no menstruation for five years; return of menstruation at thirtieth day of treatment; continued regularly ever since during three years.

Mrs. C., æt. 42, eight years without menstruation; return at fourteenth day of treatment; now regular during five months.

Miss C., æt. 22, no menstruation for eight months; return at close of sixtieth day of treatment; regular now for four months.

Miss A., æt. 26, irregular; missing for two or three months, and then menstruating irregularly for two or three months. No flow for two months. Menstruated at nineteenth day of treatment, and regular during thirteen months ever since.

I had at one time intended to give, in the first edition of this work, a full list of all my cases, with the results, but what were easy to do in definite maladies like typhoid fever becomes hard in cases such as I here relate. In the fever the statistics are simple—patients die or get well; but in cases of nervous exhaustion, so called, it is impossible to state accurately the number of partial recoveries, or, at least, to define usefully the degrees of gain. For these reasons I have not attempted to furnish full statistics of the large number of cases I have treated.

The relapses into bad health after complete cure

have been very rare; but, of course, there have been many instances in which I have merely amended the health, without perfectly restoring it. Yet even in these the examples of entire falling back into the old state have not been discouragingly numerous, while, on the other hand, I can count a large number of women who have been rescued by my treatment after all else had failed, and who have ever since enjoyed the most absolute and useful vigor of mind and body.

I do not doubt that the statements I have made will give rise in some minds to that distrust which the relation of remarkable cures so naturally excites; and this I cannot blame. Every physician can number in his own practice more or less of just such cases as I have described, and every medical man of large experience knows that many of these women are to him sources of anxiety or of therapeutic despair so deep that after a time he gets to think of them as destined irredeemably to a life of imperfect health.

I have been happy in the fact that both in private practice and at the Infirmary for Nervous Disease, my cases have of necessity been constantly under the eyes of trained and watchful observers, to whose skill and care I am indebted for many of the thermometric and other details of my cases, and who have come at last to be amply satisfied by repeated experience of the exceptional value of the treatment which I now leave to the judgment of the larger jury of my medical brothers.

INDEX.

Advantages of seclusion in emotional cases, 36.
Alcoholism in the production of fat, 19.
American race, peculiarities of, 18.
Anæmia accompanying loss of fat, 18.
Anæmia in emotional exhaustion, 29.
Anæmia produced by dyspepsia, 26.
Anæmia produced by malaria, 27.
Anæmia with accumulation of fat, 20.
Anæmic fat cases, 76.
Asthenopia, 88.

Bauer on the production of fat, 20.
Beard and Rockwell on induction current, 71.
Bleeding causing deposit of fat, 20.
Blood in its relation to fat, 23.
Bowditch on weight at different ages, 14.

Case of emotional exhaustion, 27.

Cases of local pain, with treatment, 95.
Cases of exhaustion dependent upon anæmia, 32.
Cases, emotional, 27.
Cases of rise in temperature from electricity, 66.
Cases, anæmic, fat, 76.
Climate affecting weight, 17.
Cod-liver oil, 79.
Comparison of Americans and English, 18.
Constipation, treatment of, 77.

Dietetics, 73.
Diet-list (cases reported), 84.
Digestion, weak (rest in), 47.
Dyspepsia preventing assimilation, 26.
Dyspepsia producing anæmia, 26.

Electricity, 32.
Electricity, manner of giving, 65.
Electricity elevating temperature, 65.
Electricity affecting temperature, 66–71.
Emotional cases, 27.
Emotional cases, seclusion in, 36.
Exercise, rest or tonics, 39.
Exercise, when needed, 41.

INDEX.

Exertion, over-, bad effects of, 42.
Exhaustion, nervous, 27.
Exhaustion, emotional, case of, 29.
Exhaustion, dependent upon anæmia, 64.

Fat anæmic cases, 76.
Fat in its clinical relations, 11.
Fat in its relation to health, 23.
Fat in hysterical people, 19.
Fat in old people, 19.
Fat, importance of assimilation of, 11.
Fat-producing diet, 25.

Health, fat in its relation to, 23.
Holmes on hysteria, 37.
Hysterical paralysis, case of, 75.
Hysterical people, fat in, 19.

Importance of accumulation of fat, 11.
Inconstancy of amount of fat, 13.
Induction current, 64, 71.
Introduction, 9.
Iron, preparations to use, 81.

Jackson on rest, 39.

Letheby on fattening stock, 22.

Malarial poisoning producing anæmia, 27.
Malt, when to use it, 78.
Manner of giving electricity, 65.
Manner of appearance of fat, 22.
Massage, 53.
Massage, effects of, 56-62.
Massage, effects of, on surface circulation, 63.

Massage, how to employ it, 54.
Massage, influence of, on temperature, 58.
Mechanism of storing fat, 24.
Milk diet, 73.
Milk, amount used, 73, 74.
Moral medication, 45.
Morphia causing production of fat, 19-21.

Nervous exhaustion, so-called, 27.
Normal fat of human body, 12.

Over-exertion, bad effects of, 42.

Peculiarities of American race, 18.
Pollock on gain of weight in phthisis, 26.

Quality of fat in normal body, 13.
Quetelet on weight at different ages, 13.

Rest, 38, 39, 52.
Rest, character of, 43.
Rest, Jackson on, 39.
Rest, bad effects of, how to counteract them, 53.
Rest in doubtful cases, 42.
Rest in summer, 37.
Rest in weak digestion, 47.
Résumé of treatment, 77.

Season affecting weight, 15.
Seclusion, 36.
Soup as a substitute for milk, 75-79.
Stimulus, 78-80.

Strychnia, when to use it, 81.
Swedish extension, 57.
Symptoms of emotional exhaustion, 27.

Tables of temperature after massage, 59.
Temperature elevated by electricity, 65.
Temperature affected by electricity, 66–71.
Temperature affected by massage, 58, 59.

Therapeutics, 73.
Tonics, rest or exercise, 39.
Treatment, résumé of, 77.

Urine, in over-feeding, 83.

Varieties of fat, 21.

Weight affected by season, 15.
Weight affected by climate, 17.
Weight at different ages, Bowditch on, 14.
Weight in women, 15.

THE END

www.ingramcontent.com/pod-product-compliance
Ingram Content Group UK Ltd.
Pitfield, Milton Keynes, MK11 3LW, UK
UKHW020821240326
469204UK00019B/132